We are all one and the same.

Pass it on.

DANIEL DE MORAES BRANCO, MD, PHD, MBA

Spiriduality

Spiritual Initiation for Rational People

Paperback: ISBN 979–8-9890899–0-1

Cover art by Guilherme Deganello & Helton Cardoso

Printed in the USA.

spiriduality.com

*Dedicated to
Carolina and Lorenzo.*

*So they can live in a world that
has become aware of its true spiritual nature.*

We invite you to join us:

www.spiriduality.com

Content

Preface

Thanks for showing up. We've been living in a complicated world. By believing in science and technology as the primary means of learning about our reality, we've become, as podcaster Joe Rogan likes to say, "monkeys with nuclear weapons."* As we took our initial baby steps as a species in science and technology development, we became so fascinated by it that we completely lost track of our spiritual nature. No matter how far we advance our technology, we'll continue to be just savages playing with technological toys as long as we keep denying our true selves and our origins. Science will not provide all the answers we need to thrive in every realm of our lives. For that, we need to start looking inside.

This little book was written to guide the science-and-technology-minded into the realm of spirituality. We need scientists, entrepreneurs, leaders, and policymakers

---

* *The Joe Rogan Experience*, podcast, Spotify

of all kinds to see there's something more to what meets the eye in this physical world, which we believe is all that exists. The materialistic approach to understanding reality and guiding our lives will eventually destroy us. Well, not us as spiritual beings, but us as a physical civilization.

It already feels like it will inevitably be painful, with the prospects of climate change and nuclear conflict looming over us. But there's still time for us to make better choices. All we need is a little *reframing*. And that's the goal of this book: to help us all reframe our understanding of reality so we can save our world by making choices that are more spiritual in nature and less based on fear, limitation, and lack.

Thank you for joining the movement.

Daniel de Moraes Branco

Acknowledgments

It's been a long journey. While this is a short and concise book, the understanding and reasoning applied in this work are the result of decades of exploration. The only reason I went through the trouble of attending medical school, becoming a neurologist, and working as a neuroscientist was that I wanted to understand the nature of consciousness. But it was only after I left academia and allowed myself to dive into my human life experience that I was really able to start understanding what consciousness is. Because consciousness is one of those things you can only understand by experiencing.

Many of the ideas in this book have already been developed by other people. They have been reviewed and reframed by many throughout history. My goal is to organize these ideas in such a way that they will help nonspiritual people (the rational and logical and evidence-driven) become more spiritual. This is a shift that our planet and our civilization sorely need.

And because this is a collective effort, there are many people who have been part of my journey that I want to thank. Some of them have been close to me and have had a direct impact on my life. Others don't even know me or maybe have had just a short conversation with me at a conference or event. Yet they are all an important part of this story.

Thank you, my spiritual guides, who have always inspired and guided me.

Thank you, spiritual mentors of my teenage years, Fernando Stock and Neusa Ferrarini.

Thank you, my parents, for instigating spiritual curiosity in me early on in my life.

Thank you, my childhood and lifetime friends, Fabiano Finger, with whom I've had some of the most eye-opening experiences, and Tiberio Caetano, with whom I used to spend hours exploring the limits of knowledge.

Thank you, my academic advisors in neuroscience, Dr. Jaderson Costa da Costa and Dr. Alexandra Golby.

Thank you, my coaches, therapists, and therapist friends, who held my hand while I went through my spiritual discovery journey, especially Marcus Regueira, Edna Lúcia de Andrade and Katja Rapp.

Thank you, pioneers of consciousness as an academic discipline:

- The community behind *Toward a Science of Consciousness* (now *The Science of Consciousness*), which I joined in several conferences on the subject and which helped break the stigma around it, paving the way for a true science of consciousness. Special thanks to David Chalmers, Stuart Hameroff, and Deepak Chopra.
- Donald Hoffman and his pioneering work, which makes the case for consciousness being more fundamental than space-time.
- Bernardo Kastrup and his contributions to analytic idealism.
- Curt Jaimungal and his amazing *TOE* (*Theories of Everything*) YouTube channel.

Thank you, great channelers and promoters of interdimensional wisdom, including but not limited to:
- Darryl Anka and Bashar
- Reuben Langdon and his amazing work with the *Interview with E.D.* community
- Sara Landon and the Council
- Shaun Swanson and Ishuwa
- Wieteke Koolhof and Arjun
- Aaron Abke and his *Law of One* YouTube series
- Esther Hicks and Abraham
- Alex Ferrari and his *Next Level Soul* YouTube channel
- Jay Anderson and his Project Unity, who's one of the prominent voices associating the UAP phenomena with consciousness

- Chris Lehto, who's been breaking the stigma around anomalous aerial phenomena as a retired F-16 pilot

PART I

Reframing Reality

1. Spirituality Is Not about Faith

For most people, spirituality is a matter of faith. Even for those who are not religious but see themselves as spiritual, spirituality usually still comes from some sort of belief (in "something greater," in a "greater force" in nature or in the universe, or, simply, in "Source"). These beliefs are all great ways to help us connect with the spiritual nature of reality and the spiritual aspect of ourselves. For many spiritual people, it is not even a matter of believing; they can *feel* the spiritual reality in their core.

Yet, for many others, particularly the more science-minded, building an understanding of and a connection with spirituality from a starting point of belief—in other words, believing *before* seeing or with no *evidence*—just seems wrong and unacceptable. I was, and to a great extent, still am, such a person. I don't believe that believing should be the basis for anything. (Or maybe I should say I don't *think*, because disbelief is just another type of belief.)

If you want to understand the nature of reality (and thus the nature of the world, the nature of spirituality, and the interconnection between the two), you have to let go of your beliefs and open yourself to new possibilities.

Instead of operating within a framework of belief (which excludes from your possibilities whatever contradicts that belief), I invite you to review the entirety of your beliefs, particularly the most ingrained ones (like, for example, the belief that you *are* your physical body), to start operating from a place of curiosity and open-mindedness.

Beliefs are a complicated matter. As much as our materialistic and scientistic culture pushes us to not believe in anything other than scientific evidence and forces us to base our decisions, judgments, and assessments solely on this sort of evidence, it is virtually impossible to live a life and make any decisions in it without believing in something, even if that belief is in the *fundamental existence of matter*. For example, we've been choosing as a society to assume that everything we can touch is real, and that, conversely, everything each one of us *feels* is not as real (it doesn't have object existence). That the brain exists (or so we believe), but whatever we feel is just a by-product of the brain. And that type of belief (which is actually just a choice, a belief *we've chosen* to have) impacts all sorts of decisions we make in life, from the gifts we give to how we write our laws to whether or not we choose to engage in disputes, wars and conflict.

All reasoning, no matter how simplistic, is based on one or more assumptions. And assumptions are no different than *working beliefs*. For example, most people simply assume that the material world exists. It seems obvious enough, right? We can see it, smell it, feel it. We experience it. We believe that because we can experience it, it is real. But what is more real, the world that we experience or the experience of the world? If I choose to adopt the assumption or belief that the world is real just because I can experience it, couldn't I just as easily choose to adopt the assumption or belief that the experience and the experiencer are real, just because I'm able to project a world into that experience? In other words, how can I know (physical) reality is real when all I know about it comes only from my experience of it?

That might sound like a silly question (because both the world and my experience of it could be real), but it's not. In one scenario, our bodies have objective existence in a material world where matter is capable of generating consciousness. In the other scenario, it is consciousness that has objective existence, the material world being just a creation or projection of consciousness. In this case, matter does not produce consciousness; rather, it's the opposite. And finding out which of the two possibilities is the correct—or more correct—one is extremely difficult.

Because it is difficult, we've decided as humanity to take the pragmatic approach: it doesn't matter if the mountain lion is real or if it is a projection of a deeper reality; what really matters is that that mountain lion, real or not, can put an end to my experience of reality (i.e., my life). Well, if a mountain lion can end my conscious experience, it has to be more real than my conscious experience of it. Right? Despite seeming such an obvious reasoning, that the mountain lion is real is still just an assumption and a belief. An example of a different assumption would be that we live in the "Matrix" or some other sort of simulation where we are made to believe the world—and mountain lions—are real.

Most people take the assumption that the material world exists for granted; they treat it as a *fundamental truth*. And not only do most people believe in the material world's existence but science itself is rooted in that very assumption. Moreover, science is *limited* by that assumption, because the assumption prevents scientists from studying or at least trying to understand anything that is nonmaterial or has a nonmaterial base. It goes even further: science simply *assumes* that nonmaterial phenomena (like consciousness, for example), have a material basis. As we will discuss later in this book, the idea that it is the brain that produces consciousness and not the other way around is just that: an idea based on a materialistic *assumption* (not a fact).

There are good reasons to believe in the material world and in science and in everything that results from it. One is that it works. Science simply works! It supports technologies that are really useful and often make our lives better. There are historical reasons, too, considering how much wrongdoing and injustice have been done in the name of all sorts of faiths and beliefs. For reasons like that, I decided early on in my life, when I was still a child, that I wanted to become a scientist. And so I did. I became a neuroscientist and a neurologist. I believed I would find the answers I was looking for by following the methods of science. And I still believe in the scientific method—or rather, because this book is not about faith or believing, I *think* or I have good reasons to *assume* that the scientific method works.

Yet, despite all the success of the scientific method, science, matter, space-time, and technology do not compose the full story. There's much more to our existence and our reality than meets the eye (or our scientific instruments). That which we cannot see with our eyes or measure with our instruments is the realm of spirituality. My intent with this little book is to introduce you to that realm without asking you to believe in anything different at all from what you already believe (or disbelieve).

2. The Limits of Neuroscience

There was a time when I saw the brain as the ultimate computer, one capable of generating consciousness. As an electrical engineering student in the early 1990s in southern Brazil, I had a job as a research assistant designing computer microchips. A good friend of mine from high school was also doing his undergraduate work in electrical engineering and computer science, but his research was in neural networks (a discipline that would eventually evolve to be universally referred to as *artificial intelligence*). It was by engaging with this friend, Tiberio, in deep philosophical conversations that I started thinking of the brain as this marvelous computer that was capable of producing consciousness.

At some point around that time, I made the decision to study consciousness as a scientific discipline. Growing up in a place and a time when no university disciplines on consciousness existed, the best career move I could find was going to medical school. As a neurologist, I figured, I would be able to do brain research and explore the underpinnings of how the brain generates consciousness. I changed majors to study medicine instead, and spent the entire six years of medical school (medical school is an undergraduate course of study in Brazil) developing brain mapping research for epilepsy surgery planning. My research involved several scientific techniques, including electrical cortical stimulation, current clamping in brain slices, and functional magnetic resonance imaging (fMRI). Eventually, I moved to the States, accepting a two-year research followship as a postdoctoral neuroscientist in presurgical brain mapping at Harvard. By the end of my fellowship, I had received an offer to serve in a dual appointment as professor of neuroradiology at Cornell University and the Memorial Sloan Kettering Cancer Center in New York City. However, as I'll explain later, by that time I had already concluded that I was never going to learn about consciousness by studying the brain in such a dogmatic environment as academia. I turned that offer down and switched careers, but that's a story for later in this book.

Electrical cortical stimulation may sound kind of gross, but it's such an important technique. It essentially consists of applying little electrical shocks to a patient's brain while the patient is awake, with their brain exposed during surgery. (Alternatively, a grid of electrodes can be placed under the skull for stimuli to be applied in between surgeries, also while the patient is awake.) The idea is to observe what happens to the patient's body (an involuntary limb movement, for example) or what the patient reports (a sensation or a feeling) for each applied stimulus, essentially showing what each stimulated section of the brain does. Just the application of a small electric shock can give the patient a different sensorial—

in other words, conscious—experience, such as a certain smell or the feeling of déjà vu. This is similar to the consciousness-altering phenomenon elicited by other brain-altering mechanisms such as psychedelics, which can chemically change one's conscious experience entirely.

A more palatable approach to brain mapping is functional MRI (fMRI). By using fMRI, the researcher can noninvasively study the brains of patients to map the brain areas involved with several functions, such as language understanding, speech formation, memory encoding, bodily movements, and much more. The result is a neat MRI picture of the brain overlayed by colorful blobs showing which areas of the brain are involved with a given function.

At first glance, these techniques seem to completely corroborate the idea that the brain is a fabulous consciousness-generating machine, or at least show that it is directly connected to nonmeasurable conscious experiences such as love or physical pain. But as intriguing as brains may sound to the uninitiated, the truth is that playing with them tells us absolutely nothing about how the brain generates consciousness, if it does at all. Tinkering with the brain can potentially tell us how the brain *works*, but not how consciousness *happens* or how or where it takes place.

We know that certain areas of the brain are associated with certain conscious experiences. The primary sensory area in the parietal lobe, for example, is directly associated with touch perception. The visual area in the occipital lobe is directly associated with vision (or the conscious experience of seeing). So, yes, there is a correlation between brain activity and conscious experience, but correlation is all it is. The challenge is that we have absolutely no idea how that association plays out. A correlation between two phenomena doesn't necessarily explain either phenomenon. All it tells us is that somehow, they're associated. A correlation between brain function and conscious experience doesn't automatically prove that the brain generates consciousness. From a purely correlative perspective, it could be just the opposite. It could be that the brain is generated by consciousness.

We also know that the neural networks in different areas of the brain are structured in different ways, but we don't have a clear understanding of how different neural structures develop different conscious experiences. Many structures don't even seem to be involved with consciousness at all (separating those that do and those that don't is one of the main purposes of the transsurgical cortical stimulation described earlier). And even if we could tell which neuronal structures generate each type of conscious experience, that still would not reveal the nature of consciousness.

Here's an example. Humans have five senses, all arguably generated by the brain. Now let's say, hypothetically, there's a person with a genetic mutation who claims to have a sixth sense. This person supposedly has developed new organic sensors in her body capable of perceiving, say, magnetic fields. Somehow that person can tell where north is by just *feeling* it. She may try to explain the experience to us, saying that feeling north is like feeling a "colorful pull" in her body—not quite like feeling acceleration and not like seeing either. It's something entirely different, a truly new sense. No matter how much she explains it, we can't quite make sense of what it feels like to feel north. At some point, scientists throw in the towel and decide to stop trying to understand how it feels. Out of frustration, one scientist claims that knowing what the experience of feeling north feels like is completely irrelevant, and it only matters that we can *measure* that new sense directly in the brain. Right afterward, some scientists decide to name the phenomenon "magnitision" and start rolling up their sleeves to study the new sixth sense.

While the scientific studies of magnitision would produce exactly the same types of results as those for other senses (i.e., brain maps with blobs pointing to magnitision areas in the brain, awake patients reporting the feeling of magnitision as they undergo cortical [brain] electric stimulation during awake surgery, etc.), the *experience* of having magnitision as a sense would remain alien to the rest of us who don't have that sense, including the scientists. Magnitision would represent an entirely new type of *qualia*.

Qualia is the name philosophers have given to an element of subjective conscious experience. (Technically, *qualia* is plural while *quale* is singular, but I'm treating *qualia* as grammatically singular here, as *data* sometimes is). Despite our having only five senses, which are processed by the brain, the diversity of qualia we can experience as conscious beings doesn't seem to be limited. A typical human conscious experience can include the qualia of seeing the sun setting (a sense) plus hearing kids playing in the distance (a sense) plus touching the rock we're sitting on (a sense) plus a blissful feeling of connecting with nature (not a sense) plus the pain of a cactus thorn we recently came in contact with (pain is a sense, a variation of touch) plus imagining how that sunset would look on Mars (arguably not a sense even if it's based on our senses) plus an infinitude of sensations (sensorial or not), all at the same time!

A spiritually enlightening experience is also a type of qualia that many times can't be explained in words because it is so unusual and unrelated to the physical world. Describing qualia is akin to describing a dream: you only know it when you experience it. Just like the rainbow has infinite colors that our brains interpret as seven, the qualia in conscious experience is also infinite, even if our brains reduce those experiences into countable and relatable ones. Likewise, we're able to feel a myriad of emotions, but we only have formal names for some of them. Because of that, most of us would agree that it is practically impossible to explain to a dog, which also has five senses, what it feels like to be human; the dog would have to go through the human experience to get the actual picture.

Going back to our hypothetical sixth sense, scientists would obviously be interested in studying the brain of the individual experiencing magnitision. Perhaps fMRI would be out of question because the individual experiencing magnitision might be intolerant to the strong magnetic fields in the MRI scanner. But by applying electrical stimuli, scientists might be able to pinpoint the exact location of magnitision in her brain, perhaps only to find out it has no discernible physical characteristics compared to other brain areas, or that it has slightly different neural structures. It doesn't really matter. Whatever scientists discovered, we'd still be clueless about how objective physical neural networks actually generate this subjective conscious experience.

Explaining a subjective, conscious experience by simply correlating it with physical, objective brain structures would remain unworkable. We could perhaps ascertain the brain area or the neural structure that produced magnitision, but we would not be able to tell what magnitision felt like just by looking at the physical structure. For us to know that, we'd need to *experience* it ourselves. No wealth of scientific data could show us what having magnitision feels like. And even if we could infer that magnitision feels similar to vision, say, because the underlying neural structures are similar, the fact remains that we only know how vision feels because we've consciously experienced it ourselves. Otherwise, we'd be at a complete loss of understanding.

That which can be described by science but cannot be really understood unless experienced is what I call spirituality. You don't need a new belief to realize spirituality exists. You only need to be a conscious being.

3. Defining Spirituality

One of the main challenges with spirituality is properly defining it. For the purposes of this book, we will refer to spirituality as everything that belongs to the subjective realm of consciousness. The central idea of this book is that we are spiritual beings by nature simply because we're capable of having conscious experiences. Things that we usually call "spiritual experiences" (faith, visions, premonitions, etc.) all happen in consciousness. Here, I'm expanding the concept to include all conscious experience, mystic or not, in the definition of spirituality.

The idea is quite simple, actually. The laws of physics do not even suggest that consciousness exists, let alone explain it. We have absolutely no scientific basis to infer the existence of consciousness from matter. There are no known mechanisms or theories for how matter generates consciousness or becomes conscious. Yet, we all know we are conscious beings with conscious experiences. If matter can be conscious and we have no scientific explanation for how that happens, attributing consciousness to another realm—the spiritual—is completely reasonable.

One might ask: Isn't it possible that current natural laws won't explain consciousness but future ones will? Yes, that is a possibility, but I'm not convinced it is that simple, for two reasons:

1. Regardless of how much science will explain for us in the future, consciousness is not really something you *explain*; it is something you *experience*. The scientific method, as it is defined today, isn't likely to be able to probe that experiential nature of reality to develop a thorough understanding of what consciousness is unless it is experienced directly. In that sense, science and instruments are useless in explaining it.

2. If we succeed in scientifically explaining (and experiencing) the association of matter with consciousness that allows for brains to be conscious, that might be exactly the moment when we discover the natural laws of the spiritual realm. I say this because I don't really think consciousness is supernatural; quite the opposite! Consciousness is as natural as it gets. We have firsthand experience of it. It is the most undeniable reality of our lives! It just happens that how it works is still unexplained. With that explanation, an entire realm of possibilities and realities might be waiting for us.

I'm proposing in this book that being conscious beings is what makes us spiritual beings. It's as simple as that. No special faith or belief is required. You're spiritual in nature just because you are a conscious being.

From that perspective, we're all spiritual in nature. There's nothing we need to do to become more or less spiritual. Spiritual *is* our nature. There's no escaping that. Now, what we can choose is a more—or less—spiritual *life*.

When it comes to spiritual life, it is also worth discussing what spirituality is *not*. For the purposes of this book, spirituality is not about being good or bad. A good person is not necessarily more spiritualized than a bad person, however good and bad are defined. It is not about being right or wrong, either. It is not about being spiritually "evolved," let alone being faithful or religious (arguably, one can be very religious and not very spiritual, and vice versa). For the purposes of this discussion, being spiritual is simply being aware of your conscious—and, thus, spiritual—nature. The more you realize you exist beyond your body, the more spiritual you become. It doesn't require any faith or specific beliefs. It only requires you to accept and understand who you truly are, which is obvious: *you are a conscious being whose consciousness does not exist in matter*, because there's no scientific evidence that consciousness exists locally in matter. It's as simple as that. (*Locally* is a technical term to describe a phenomenon that happens in specific coordinates of space and time.)

But how can I be sure consciousness does not exist in matter (in my brain)? you might ask. To which I would reply: How can you be sure it does? If there's no proof that matter can create consciousness, the choice is yours to make. Either your brain is creating consciousness or consciousness is creating your brain[†]. There's no way to know for sure. You've been living your life *assuming* that the brain creates consciousness; now you can simply make the choice to live your life based on a different assumption. Look around you. *Everything* that is man-made was created in consciousness first. Cars, phones, streets, cities, pyramids, absolutely *everything* that we manifest in this world started in consciousness as someone's idea. How can we tell whether that pattern isn't the same for everything else? Could the brain have been created in consciousness first, too? Could the universe? I can't really rationally argue against that idea.

Remember, you are a spiritual being by nature. You're conscious! That's not a choice. The only choice you have is between accepting that fact or resisting it. If you choose, you can become more and more aware of that fact of your life: that you're conscious and, thus, spiritual. And that's how you become more or less spiritual *in life*.

People with more spiritual lives live as if they were limitless and unbound by matter. They're not afraid of dying, they're not fear-driven, and they won't engage in conflict and polarization, just because none of that makes

---

[†] Technically, it could also be the case that something else creates both the brain and consciousness. For the purposes of this book, however, which essentially is to challenge the assumption that consciousness is created by the brain, discussing just the alternative assumption is already plenty.

sense from a spiritual perspective. As they see it, they are not as *separated* from their spiritual nature.

Less spiritual people live as if matter is all that exists, as if life in matter is *separate* from life in spirit. They form attachments to material things, leading to pain, conflict, and suffering, because they see reality as a by-product of matter rather than of consciousness. They will attach not only to material stuff but also to all sorts of less-spiritual concepts, like titles, status, their own ego identity (take away from them their career or their country and they can no longer make sense of who they are), and even attachment to other people (believing they're gone when they die, for example). That has nothing to do with being a good or bad person. It just comes from a mistaken assumption, which is that we are ephemeral bodies with brains that somehow magically produce consciousness, and which will cease to exist when the brain dies.

We have this magical idea that our life on Earth is the "real deal," and that spiritual life only starts after death (if you believe in life after death). What I'd like you to see is that your spiritual life is happening right here and right now, by the simple fact that you are a conscious being. You are matter and you are spirit at the same time! You don't need to die to become a ghost; you already are one—a friendly one.

To help reconcile the duality of physical life vs. spiritual life, we need to revisit our understanding of reality.

4. The Duality of Reality

Ask anyone what reality is and you'll find that most people associate reality with stuff that can be touched or observed (the table, the chair, our bodies, other peoples' bodies, fire, rain, our planet, the universe, etc.). It was science that showed us there are things much more real than we can perceive with our limited senses. Of the entire electromagnetic spectrum, for example, we can see but a tiny fraction. Most light in the universe (infrared, ultraviolet, X-rays, radio, microwave, etc.) is invisible to us. Science has helped us understand that reality is complex and big, but also orderly. The laws of physics are taken as the fundamental rules of our reality. Yet that's far from the whole story.

The word *laws* in this phrase is old terminology. Today, physicists prefer to use the terms *theories* or *models*, because past developments have taught us that our "laws" can be incomplete, that there's always another layer to the onion of reality. Physicists have been looking for a TOE (a theory of everything) for a long time, and my take is that a theory of *everything* will not be found until we start taking into consideration *everything* that exists, including consciousness and our conscious experience of the world (seems obvious to me). But I'll continue to refer to "laws" of physics throughout the book, because even if we understand that our theories are incomplete, the underlying assumption continues to be that the world is fundamentally governed by one or more very specific rules, or "laws." The common understanding is that we just haven't fully discovered them yet.

These laws support our understanding of what most of us perceive as third-person reality. But there are two (mostly) indisputable types of reality: *third-person reality* and *first-person reality*. Third-person reality is what almost everyone understands as being real. It is the reality we can all agree upon. *This chair is here and we can all touch it; thus it is real.* Third-person reality needs no further explanation. Everybody knows what I'm talking about. If I crash my car, that's real; if I watch a game, that's real; if I break my arm, that's real; if I die, that's real. Even if we live in a polarized world full of frequently fabricated information these days, we all agree on the reality that exists underneath it. That's third-person reality. Generally, we don't question its existence (at some level).

Third-person reality is also the realm of science. By using ever more complex tools, science's greatest accomplishment has been to expand our comprehension of third-person reality by generating all sorts of evidence that, despite not being readily experienced by our senses, we can all agree is true. We run clinical trials to prove that a drug works, so we welcome that drug into our third-person reality. It becomes a thing. We develop ever more powerful telescopes to see further and further away. So, because now we can see them, all of those galaxies also become part of our common understanding of reality.

Third-person reality is irrefutable for anyone who has measured it. Not even the most spiritualized person will say it doesn't exist—on some level, at least.

Then we have first-person reality. First-person reality is everything we *feel*. Let's say you break your arm in third-person reality. Your doctors can look at an X-ray and agree that your arm really is broken, and they will agree on a specific description of that fractured bone. But the *pain* of that broken arm is all yours to enjoy! You can't prove to anyone else that you are or aren't in pain. Not only that, other people (the third parties in your third-person reality) cannot and will not agree on a specific description of your pain. *Because pain has no description, not really.* You can try to explain it, but one can only understand pain by *feeling* it. If you know what pain is, it means you've already felt it. Otherwise, you'd have no clue, no matter how well somebody tried to describe pain to you.

Let that sink in for a minute. Try to explain to an AI robot that you are feeling pain. How well do you think a being who has never felt pain can understand what pain is? *Is that even real?* your AI friend might even ask you. Even the concept of *feeling* would be otherworldly for it. Now, let's say your AI friend is a scientist (it is an intelligent robot designed to dig up scientific evidence of all kinds).

And it wants proof from you that you have this thing called pain. Would you be able to provide any?

Doctors handle this with their patients in a certain way. When a patient says they're in pain, the doctor will ask: *On a scale from one to ten, how bad is your pain?* It sounds so primal and unsophisticated. Why can't the doctor just use some sort of device to measure pain? Because pain isn't measurable! It is not that we haven't yet developed the technology to measure pain. No! The answer is that pain really isn't a thing. Pain simply isn't *real*, at least not in third-person reality. You can decide for yourself whether or not pain is real (Have you felt it?), but if it is real, it's real only in first-person reality, and only for you. In third-person reality, it simply doesn't exist.

The only reason a human doctor asks you about pain is because she herself has also felt it, so you can both agree it is something that exists. But if your doctor is a nonsentient robot (because sentient robots might arguably be conceived as well), it will only ask you about your pain because, being a smart cookie, it has come to the conclusion that when it asks patients about their "pain," it can correlate the answer with the severity of the problem. It has no real clue what pain is. It has simply learned the *science* of pain. It has learned how to measure a *correlate* of pain. (This notion of *correlates* is important, and we will use it again later on.)

First-person reality is irrefutable for whomever has experienced it. Not even the most materialistic person will say it doesn't exist (at least, to some degree).

First-person reality is a reality that only sentient beings can access. It is not a material reality, and there's no scientific way to prove it exists. In July of 2022, a Google engineer was fired after claiming an AI model developed by the company was sentient.[‡] Google's answer was that there is no evidence that the model was sentient, but the company never really explained what kind of evidence would show it to be sentient, if that were the case. In our daily lives, we simply *assume* other people are sentient because we don't really have hard evidence to the contrary. The evidence the Google engineer had was pretty much the same as we have when we assume other people are sentient: we're able to engage in meaningful interactions with other sentient beings. That's it. There's no scientific proof for sentience, as there isn't for pain.

Now, some might ask: Isn't pain directly and functionally attributed to a series of neurons/synapses/C fibers firing? And I ask you back: Is it? Because, if it is, we don't really understand, based on the entirety of our current knowledge of nature, how that is so. For all we know scientifically, a series of neurons is not fundamentally different from a series of copper wires. We know we can use copper wires or gold wires to build computers and machines that sense the environment around them and react to it. Now, could those machines be feeling pain, or anything at all? We just assume they don't, but we don't

---

[‡] Nico Grant, "Google Fires Engineer Who Claims Its A. I. Is Conscious," *New York Times*, July 23, 2022, https://www.nytimes.com/2022/07/23/technology/google-engineer-artificial-intelligence.html.

know that for sure. Likewise, I can only assume that you, dear reader, feel pain, but I don't know that as scientific fact. For all I know, you could just be *claiming* to feel pain. The only reason I believe you feel pain is because I feel it, too. But that's not really a scientific parameter. If a group of neurons can feel pain, we still have no clue how that happens.

I'm not saying we can't figure out how to build something that feels pain, if all that takes, after all, is just a bunch of neurons grouped together. What we can't figure out is how the experience of pain *emerges* from neuronal activity. Not only that, but when and if we learn how that happens, we will necessarily need a new set of physical laws, because no current law of physics suggests the experience of pain (or any kind of qualia) by matter, no matter how well-structured or organized it gets (be it in the form of neurons or copper wires).

For all we scientifically know about nature, there's no mechanism that allows matter to have feelings. There's something else, which is the *agent* that feels the pain, and there are no reasons or scientific subsidies at all to assume that the agent is material (matter-based). Neurons and the information flowing through them do allow for the conscious experience of pain, since an increase in pain nerve activity correlates with an increased experience of pain, but that nerve activity happens in third-person physical reality while the experience of pain itself is nonmaterial and not reachable to science. Our brains could well be just creations of consciousness that allow it to perceive physical reality, our bodies working as the instruments that consciousness uses to probe a physical reality not of our own spiritual nature.

To introduce you to spirituality, the only thing I need you to "believe" is that your (first-person experience of) pain is real. I'm not even talking about your soul hurting or anything intangible like that. I'm talking about your broken arm. That's all I need. If you don't believe your pain is real when you break your arm (and some scientists actually don't), you are a lost cause. You can stop reading this book and ask for a refund! If the bookstore won't give you one, send me an email at contact@spiriduality.com and I'll make sure to pay you the full amount back, even if I only received a fraction of what you paid. Just please have some intellectual integrity and give up anesthesia next time you have surgery, will you?

OK, it's only us now, pain believers!

So far, so good. I don't think anybody in the remaining group is raising eyebrows yet. The problem starts here: If pain is not defined in third-person reality, which reality is real, third-person or first-person? In other words, which one is more *fundamental*?

By "fundamental," I mean that which is most necessary for everything else to take place. If consciousness is generated by the brain, then the brain (i.e., matter) is more fundamental than consciousness. Conversely, if the brain (and all matter) is a creation in consciousness, then consciousness is more fundamental than matter. It comes first as a necessity for reality to exist.

At this point you may be asking, *Why do we need two realities at all? Pain exists in the only reality that exists, which is third-person reality, the real, material world. We just haven't developed the technology to understand it yet.*

While I'd agree we don't need two or multiple realities to explain pain, we can't really explain it in third-person reality terms. In other words, pain (or love, or hate, or vision, or touch, or any form of qualia, really) cannot be demonstrated to exist scientifically. And if qualia can't be found or demonstrated scientifically, then there's more to reality than science can reveal to us. That's first-person reality: a reality that can't be probed scientifically (because of its nature, not because of our lack of technological prowess). To put it another way, science, as a third-person reality method, is incapable of dealing with phenomena it wasn't designed to deal with in the first place.

There's a lot to unpack here. And that's what we're going to do in the next chapter.

5. Spiri*duality*: The Drama of Conscious Beings

Being a conscious being kind of sucks. Think about it. A teacup is never concerned about its existence. It happily just exists to fulfill its purpose. Happily? Can a teacup have feelings? I have no clue! Maybe it does; maybe it doesn't. I can't think of a scientific experiment to answer that question. The teacup doesn't present any behavioral correlates of consciousness, that's for sure, and it wouldn't scream in pain if it got chipped. Even if it did somehow show signs of feeling pain, how could we be sure what it actually felt? Does an ant feel tired after carrying a big load on its back? Would there be any reason for us to even postulate that it does other than the fact that we ourselves feel that way when we do the same? Does sugar taste the same for an ant as it does for us? How translatable are the physical correlates of our own conscious experiences to other organisms and structures? Or to other people?

Do you, dear reader, have feelings? Again, I can't tell! If you are a bot scanning the Internet for content, you probably aren't feeling anything at all while reading this. If you are a human being, I might *assume* you feel something. I can't prove it scientifically, but I can assume it is the case, based on the fact that I have feelings myself. That you have feelings, however, is my own belief about you, which can't be proven. It is not a scientific fact. From a strictly scientific perspective, believing that you, a fellow human being, have feelings and sentience is a matter of faith, a faith based on my own direct experience of being sentient, too.

So, why do we need this "duality" of two perceived types of realities (third and first-person)? Essentially, we need it because we're conscious beings. This is the duality we need to face and make sense of as conscious (spiritual) beings interacting with each other through a materialistic framework. It is our *spiriduality*, because it's a duality that exists only because of our spiritual and conscious nature. Were we not conscious or sentient, we wouldn't need to bother with those questions. We could just go on with our lives. Happily. Just like the teacup. But conscious beings we are, for better or worse. It is because we have consciousness that we can also have conscious experiences of pain, love, hate, and joy. Our consciousness is our window into the world. Then again, which world? Third-person or first-person?

Before this gets too crazy, let me make something clear: there's only one world, one existence, one reality. There aren't really two realities. Still, we have a duality. Because we have an outside world that almost everybody agrees is out there, and we each have an inner world, which almost everybody agrees is within each one of us. Others can't see or probe our first-person account of reality. The only way to experience being me is by being me. The only way to experience being you is by being you. The only way to experience being a dolphin that uses echolocation is by being a dolphin that uses echolocation. From a third-person, scientific perspective, we can learn all about echolocation mechanics and the underlying physics. But to know how it *feels* to be a dolphin using echolocation, you would have to become that dolphin.

Now, one might argue that we could potentially create brain implants in the future that would give us the experience of echolocation. While that might be true, it still wouldn't solve the duality, for you'd need to wear the implant and experience it to *know* what that reality felt like. You could understand how that implant worked, but you couldn't really tell what it felt like to wear it until you went through the experience. Understanding the physics of the implant would not inform you about the experience or the qualia of using the implant. No outside data or understanding or knowledge or intelligence could replace the very act of going through that experience.

Think of a blind scientist. She might know everything there is to know about light—how the light refracts, how the different wave frequencies create each color—but she won't understand what a color is and how it feels to experience red if she can't see it, no matter how knowledgeable or smart she is. It is not a matter of technology or scientific acumen. Science and technology simply cannot fully inform about the experience. It has to be lived.

Therefore, while we probably only have one fundamental reality—in other words, we don't need multiple realities to explain all the things we experience—there are certainly at least two ways to understand and make sense of it: from a consensus (scientific, third-person) perspective and from a personal (experiential, first-person) perspective. That's important! That duality exists and we don't have the means, scientific or otherwise, to tell which one is more true or more correct or more valid. Yet, humanity has made a very clear choice to pick consensus reality as the one and true reality. And that choice has been hugely impactful, shaping our entire worldview as a species. In my view, however, the greatest fallacy of our time is believing that the scientific, objective approach to understanding reality is the only one that has merit and holds water. If anything, I'd like to suggest that it is just the opposite.

6. A Problem of Physics and Measurement

As a neuroscientist in the early 2000s at Brigham and Women's Hospital in Boston, I had a very specific job: to map the brains of patients who were being prepared to undergo epilepsy or brain tumor surgery. The basic idea was that I'd instruct patients to execute determined tasks related to memorizing words, patterns, and scenery pictures while I acquired MRI images of their brains.

Our scientific understanding of the brain is still extremely limited. We have almost no means or technology to "fix" anything in the brain. Most of the time, our only option is to remove dysfunctional areas. Cutting off brain pieces is what neurosurgeons do most often. Because some areas of the brain are more sensitive, more "important," than others, my job was to use functional MRI, as described in chapter 2, to map the location of certain sensitive areas of each candidate patient's brain, areas responsible for language, memory, and other functions.

It was an amazing thing. By using the technique, I could identify the exact location in the brain of the areas responsible for moving the patient's fingers, for example, or for making them feel touch in different areas of their body. Removing those areas would have rendered the patient finger-motionless or insensitive to touch. At first glance, that seems like a huge confirmation that *we are our brains*. Remove one part of the brain and you lose the conscious experience related to it, be it the conscious command of a part of the body or the ability to perceive its existence—and thus, perceive the world. Conversely, a person who loses a limb but whose brain remains intact can continue to feel that limb, even when it's no longer there. What more evidence would anyone need? Clearly, consciousness is produced by the brain, right?

Well, not so fast. My maps certainly showed a measurement of neural activity that correlated with conscious experience. If an area of the brain was lit up on the map, that person was surely reporting a related experience of moving their finger or feeling it. Yet, we don't really know how it is that the electrical activity in a bunch of neurons generates conscious experience. That is not even a challenge neuroscience is trying to address. The problem goes much deeper. If you take the laws of physics as we know them today, you will not find the barest indication that a clump of matter, regardless of its properties or how well-structured it is, even if it is as organized as a brain, can generate such a thing as conscious experience.

From a strictly scientific point of view, consciousness is *supernatural*. It simply doesn't exist. Some scientists may give voice to the idea that consciousness is an "epiphenomenon," which is like saying that consciousness just "happens", that it is simply a by-product of third-person consensus reality and should not be taken as a real thing. This is an easy way around the issue that doesn't help anyone or explain anything. Yet, despite being supernatural by definition, a phenomenon beyond scientific understanding or the known laws of nature, consciousness is probably the one phenomenon that couldn't be more real and present for each one of us. Moreover, it is a phenomenon that *everyone believes*. With the exception of a few intellectual eccentrics, nobody disbelieves the existence of their own consciousness.

The only proof we have that we exist and that everything else also exists is our consciousness. Our consciousness is the ultimate reality-checking instrument. All other instruments, including every scientific instrument, only make indirect measurements of reality. The only thing that directly "measures" or probes reality, by means of directly experiencing it, is consciousness. Everything you know about yourself and the world around you only exists at a consciousness level. Further, *knowing* only happens in consciousness. Only consciousness can *know*. A computer can process and store information and knowledge, but does it really *know* the information it is storing? And since knowing only happens at the consciousness level, the world doesn't even need objective existence if consciousness can simply create the representation of that world in it. (Can it? Maybe...)

This is where lots of people are going to say that matter can indeed generate consciousness if it's organized in the right way, like in our brains. They'll argue that there's nothing wrong with the idea that the brain generates consciousness; we just don't know how it happens *yet*. And this is the moment when we pause, take a deep breath, and ask those people for a little bit of intellectual consistency. Because people (usually the ones more immersed in third-person reality) who say that conscious experience is a true physical phenomenon whose physical basis has simply not yet been discovered are likely the very same scientists who say, for example, that faster-than-light travel is impossible, because the known laws of physics won't allow it.

But if we accept consciousness, a supernatural belief by (scientific) definition, as a real and physical phenomenon that is based on still-unknown physics, we can't at the same time refute the idea of a soul, spirit, or God on the basis that those phenomena would be contrary to our current understanding of physics. It's not logical to use the currently known laws of physics to determine what can and can't be and then allow for only *certain* phenomena to exist, assuming that some future and unknown physical knowledge will explain them. Who's to decide now which phenomena future theories of physics will or will not explain?

My point is, it is totally fine for anyone to believe or disbelieve whatever they want. But a little consistency is helpful. If you're still reading this book, that's because you believe in pain. You know your arm is going to hurt when it breaks. And if you have been paying attention, dear reader, you know there's absolutely no explanation anywhere in our sciences for your conscious experience of pain. If you believe in pain, *you already believe in the supernatural.* It's as simple as that. So why not take advantage of the fact that you already are a believer of the supernatural and allow the spiritual in your life, too? In the end, it's all the same thing.

Now, wait a minute! you might yell at me. *Eventually our science* will *evolve and we* will *understand the nature of the conscious experience of pain, and we* will *understand how the universe creates consciousness, and everything will be clear. We believe in conscious experience (and not in ghosts, for example), because we know it exists, because we can* feel *it, and everybody else agrees, because they feel it, too.*

Very well, I'd answer. *I completely agree with you.* One day we will understand conscious experience, but there isn't really a reason to think that will happen through science, at least not through the scientific method. That's simply because first-person experience is not within the scope of the method. Consciousness is out of its scope almost by definition. When real understanding of consciousness happens, even if we're still calling it "scientific," the method will be of a different nature than the science we have today. Necessarily, it will be a science that evolved to make use of both the third- *and* first-person perspectives of the world. And who knows what other phenomena will be validated by that future method? I can't prove it (obviously), but my take is that a future science that proves conscious experience is real will also prove that our physical world in space-time is not as real as we believe it to be today.

In the end, when we finally become able to demonstrate that conscious experience is real—not its correlates, but the actual experience—we might just as well discover that consciousness is more fundamental than matter, that there is an existence and a reality beyond space-time, and that all the truths we were so convinced about (like the idea that our brain generates consciousness) were simply completely wrong. Maybe instead of generating consciousness, our brain is simply filtering out consciousness that exists nonlocally outside of the brain. Maybe consciousness has an infinite potential for experiencing qualia, but it chooses to temporarily restrict itself to only five senses, so it can experience this human existence. Maybe we will discover and manage to experience qualia that was once beyond our wildest imagination.

Once again in history, humanity may have to go through another humility lesson, like the ones it endured when it learned that the Earth was not at the center of the universe, that the Earth was not flat, that not washing hands actually killed patients, or that nonlocality exists and that quantum entanglement really means the universe allows for "spooky actions at a distance" (an expression coined by Einstein to describe a real quantum phenomenon he didn't believe to be real). As a species, we are stubborn as hell, and we insist on believing that the latest knowledge is ultimate knowledge. We should know better by now. At any time in history, including right now, known knowledge will always need to be revisited, reframed, reinterpreted, and reunderstood. Claiming to know the truth based on current scientific knowledge is as silly as it gets. Yet we won't stop doing it.

The point when we learn consciousness is real may be the point we learn spirituality is just as real. They're actually the same thing. Because the entity that feels pain and has conscious experiences does not derive from the mechanics of a material world as we know it; it derives from a world that exists, that is natural, but is beyond matter and space-time, a world that is *spiritual*.

7. A Fundamental Choice

It is not the goal of this book to convince you that first-person realities are more fundamental than third-person ones. We just don't have the means today to tell for certain which one derives from the other. But it stands to reason that one of those realities ought to derive from the other. Either the brain generates consciousness or consciousness generates the brain (and all matter). It seems simpler to assume that we have only one base reality (or a single "theory of everything," as filmmaker Curt Jaimungal discusses on his YouTube channel), in which case either first-person reality derives from third-person reality or the other way around.

As I've insisted since the beginning of this book, believing in anything is kind of silly, anyway. We should not close our options by believing in just one of them. Leave your options open; you have nothing to lose by doing so. Be curious and explore new ideas. Don't get attached to beliefs, because eventually they'll be proven wrong. It's a recurring and time-proven principle.

As I've said before, the only thing I expect you to believe is that pain is real. If you already believe that, you're all set. You already are a spiritual person. Really. You may not see it that way yet, and it may be a long time before you really *feel* spiritual, but there's no other way around it. If you believe there's such a nonscientific and "supernatural" thing as the conscious experience of pain (or love or any type of qualia), you already have all the belief you need to build a more spiritual and happier life for yourself (also because happiness is a conscious experience, so you need to believe in first-person realities to believe in happiness anyway).

In the end, it is not even a matter of believing; it's simply a matter of choice. You don't need faith or belief in anything in particular to become spiritual. Having spirituality in your life is a *choice*.

And it's a simple one:

> 1. You may choose to understand the world from a third-person perspective, as everybody else does. Or...

> 2. You may choose to explore and understand reality from a first-person perspective, which gives you the opportunity to build an entirely different understanding of the world and your role in it.

There's no right or wrong choice, only different outcomes. The world we have today is mostly based on the first choice. It is a technologically successful world, but it fails in many other critical ways (endless wars being one example). Everything you experience in your life is a result of how you choose to interpret things and facts. We understand life through a certain prism or framework that we've internalized in our heads. It can come preformatted as religion or ideology, or you can build it from the ground up based on *first principles*, which are basic assumptions that cannot be deduced any further.

By revisiting the choice between interpreting reality from a third-person perspective or a first-person one, this book is returning to a very important first principle: the assumption that our own nature is either material or spiritual. That either the brain creates consciousness or consciousness creates the brain. This is an assumption that can't be deduced any further. The choice between first-principle assumptions means a lot. Those assumptions form the basis for the frameworks you use to interpret life and reality. Every one of your experiences in life goes through that prism, so choosing the right one for your goals in life is very important!

If you look around, it's easy to notice the consequences of choosing to see the world through a third-person lens. For starters, you're always looking for external validation. Everybody does this; have you noticed? Since they can't trust who they truly are, and all they believe themselves to be is a body or a clump of mass called *brain*, they constantly need others to validate their existence and their worth. As a result, reality becomes a huge game where each one of us plays a different role in society, often without even noticing. We end up believing we *are* the characters we play. We build our identities as beings based on our jobs, our networks, our positions among family members and friends. We keep looking for ways to feel special. When you fall into this mindset, you are no longer yourself; you become the things you own, including your status and reputation. Instead of being what you feel and know to be true on the inside, you become that which others think of you.

You already know that game, right? You cherish it. You want to "win" it. You don't want to be a loser. You start acting from a place of fear. You're afraid of what could happen to you if you lose the things you have; you become afraid of losing your job, of losing control, of dying. On a country level, you start waging wars. You don't want to lose everything you think you have, because you've become that which you have. You need power because you think you lack it. Little do you realize it's all a performance. It's not who you really are. In third-person reality, we believe we are puppets trying to survive in a world we can't control. In first-person reality, however, you realize you're the puppeteer! There, you have full control.

In first-person reality, you can decide which experiences to build to yourself. In practice, that's always the case, regardless of the choice you make. Just like every human-made thing was first conceived in consciousness, your own life with its experiences is built at your own consciousness level first. The problem with choosing to assume third-person reality creates first-person experiences is that you delegate the creation of your experiences and your own life to the rules of 3D (the three space dimensions of the physical world: height, length, and width). By your own choice, you're no longer in control. And when you're not in control, you allow for all sorts of experiences to happen to you, either positive or negative, wanted or unwanted.

When you choose 3D as ultimate reality, it's not that you don't have the power to build your own good experiences from a first-person-reality space. You're still creating your third-person reality from your first-person reality the whole time, but your consciousness space is now populated by what others have created for you, which can be positive or negative.

By making the choice to assume first-person reality is what gives life to third-person reality, you can start getting in touch with your true self. You can meditate to quiet your brain and take it out of the equation. You can be happy by just being. Happiness no longer comes from external sources, like professional or business achievements, winning whatever game or war you think you're playing in 3D, owning stuff, receiving recognition from others, power or control over others, or being at the top of whatever pyramid you've created for yourself. In first-person reality, if you want to, you can make the conscious decision to be in a good place, to be happy, to enjoy life regardless of what 3D throws at you. You learn how to appreciate nature and the universe. Everything is a sensation. Qualia is everywhere around you to be experienced. You become one with Source Consciousness and everyone else around you. You start seeing yourself in everybody else. There's no longer hate. Or fear. Only acceptance and enjoyment.

The choice is yours and only yours to make. Nobody can tell you (let alone prove) that spiritual reality doesn't exist. Conversely, nobody can prove to you that it does. That proof can only come from experiencing it directly, because spiritual reality is of an experiential nature. Just like pain. And that can be tricky, because first you need to make the decision to dedicate the time and energy to reframing your worldview and your understanding of what is really real. Only then can you start perceiving reality as such. But you already know your pain is real, right? And for all we've learned about the material world through science, pain shouldn't be real. So how difficult can it be for you to accept that the spiritual experience can be just as real as pain? You actually do know that it can. You are a spiritual and conscious being. You can feel it. Your consciousness is as spiritual and real as it gets.

Sometimes, life makes that choice for you. At the age of forty-one, while exercising in the gym, I had a fulminating heart attack (not the type that announces itself in advance in the form of angina or other symptoms). It came totally out of the blue. I had no known heart problems and no clear risk factors. The pain just came, and it kept growing and growing until I passed out. For a few minutes, I was unconscious, having a near-death experience (NDE). It was not as colorful as many others are reported to be. But it was extremely peaceful. Never in my life had I felt so much peace. Nothing mattered anymore. I no longer had an identity or a body. I had no memories. It was like I was just floating in a void and it was extremely joyful and calm, the sort of thing I had never felt before. I didn't want to come back, but eventually I did. As I returned to life, it was like a thousand drums were beating around me. That's when I realized how noisy life is.

Being alive in these biological bodies is extremely tense. Most of the time we can't tell, because we don't usually have the contrast of not having that "noise" around. All of our memories are from living in these bodies. But when you dissociate from your body's biology (which, as a matter of fact, is a rumbling machine), that's when you have access to pure peace and bliss.

For many years after that heart attack (from which I fully recovered, never to find out exactly what caused it in the first place), I always wanted to go back to that peace. It's not that I wanted to die, because there is no dying (if consciousness is more fundamental than the brain, it can always create another brain or another physical life). It was more akin to wanting to move back to that place instead of living in this one. Like changing countries, as I've done. Simple as that. Now that I knew how much better it could be, life on Earth just felt too heavy and mundane. I could no longer see it in the same way. My entire worldview changed. From their (third-person) perspective, my family members couldn't make sense of my change. But I knew, for I had experienced it firsthand. No amount of explanation was enough to make them see. I got really depressed.

As I continued through my spiritual journey, things started improving. Little by little, I stopped having that urge to move, to return to that better place. I was learning how to build that peace within me. Here, in this world. Instead of needing to change my reality by moving to a better place, I learned how to change my reality by bringing that better place into myself. As I internalized the idea that consciousness is more fundamental than matter and took action based on the choice to use that assumption, I started realizing that we're all light beings in consciousness. We all have the capacity to go through conscious experiences. We all build our own conscious realities. But for some reason, as spiritual beings, we still choose to experience the challenges of life on Earth as human beings. Those lives in human form last only a little while, though. What feels like a lifetime in space-time is just like a blink of an eye out there.

The second part of this book is about initiating you on your spiritual journey. Many people have been through this already. Actually, the whole purpose of life on Earth is to take that journey. From a spiritual perspective, everything is already solved. There are no problems or challenges. As consciousness, we are pure creative energy, which we have come to call love. In 3D reality, however, we have all of our challenges. But, if you learn how to look through the prism of first-person reality, challenges become fun, joyful, and uplifting. It is only by choosing the materialistic approach that everything becomes so heavy and tense. In the end, the only reality that exists is the one that you yourself create and experience, and it derives directly from what you choose to believe in. You are the result of your beliefs, and your beliefs are *always* your choice. The better the beliefs you choose to have, the better your life is going to be.

I'm not a spiritual master of any kind. I consider myself quite detached from the spiritual realm, actually, and still too attached to 3D (space-time/third-person) reality. But that's also a good position to be in to help build the bridge between these two realities and give a little hand to people who are still so immersed in 3D that they're unable to perceive or believe in anything else.

PART II:

Igniting Your Spiritual Life

8. Detaching from Old-School Methods

The first part of this book was not intended to be esoteric or to convey knowledge that has been kept secret until now. Quite the opposite. I mean, consciousness is seen as esoteric by many people just because it doesn't have objective existence and cannot be proven to exist by science. But the thing is that everyone already believes in consciousness (their own consciousness, anyway). So much so that people will take consciousness as scientific fact when it absolutely isn't, at least not according to our current working definition of science. Although the ideas discussed in part 1 may sound fringe, mystical, or ethereal to some extent, that is only because the very nature of consciousness can also be seen as fringe, mystical, or ethereal. But if you assume consciousness to be real, and if you choose to go further by assuming it is more real than matter, then all the ideas discussed in part 1 are just a rational derivation of that assumption. Nothing there is woo-woo.

At this point in the book, we already accept the existence of pain and consciousness. (We do, right?). We also understand that consciousness cannot be explained by third-person science, because it belongs to an experiential aspect of reality. Even though *consciousness correlates* can be studied scientifically (as I did in my days as a neuroscientist), the *knowing of how it feels to see the rainbow* is knowing limited to the consciousness realm (first-person reality).

There is also the idea that consciousness is a window into the spiritual realm, which is natural and not "supernatural," but not necessarily physical as we understand physics today. In other words, it is not restricted to the space-time-based scientific framework. The fundamental idea is that we are, first and foremost, spiritual beings, not *brains*. And that would explain why we have consciousness and experience qualia. Since our scientific theories don't explain why and how matter can experience consciousness, I like to entertain the idea that the experiential nature of reality precedes and is more fundamental than matter. Not only is this a powerful and valid idea but it's actionable. And acting on it produces real results, as any person who has been through a spiritual transformation would attest.

It is also important to stress that being *rational* doesn't automatically require being *scientific*. Quite the opposite: science is a product of reasoning, not the other way around. We learned to think before we learned to do science. If you were expecting to learn about spirituality from a scientific perspective when I said that this book was a spiritual initiation for rational people, I'm sorry to disappoint. What I meant was that you can make sense of spiritual reality and live a spiritual life by simply being rational about what your experience of the world tells you, and you can do this without making use of any type of faith or esoteric belief. You can rely solely on your own first-person experience as a conscious being to find and bring spirituality into your life.

Nobody knows how many revolutions in physics we're going to need to truly understand consciousness. As I suggested earlier, we might not even recognize science as such by the time it allows us to fully understand the nature of consciousness. And science alone might never get there. Consciousness could indeed be just beyond the possibilities of third-person description. But if that becomes possible, then the scientific method will have to be adapted to operate outside of space-time constraints. This is already the case for several controversial scientific subjects unrelated to consciousness. Even though there are solid theoretical grounds for ideas like the existence of the multiverse, parallel realities, extra dimensions (string theory comes to mind), and others, many physicists believe that those are just speculations that should not be taken seriously because they cannot be tested by the scientific method in a lab.

Despite all the success of the scientific method (for those lines of research that fall within its scope), it seems to me that forcing nature to manifest only in ways that can be tested by the scientific method—our favorite tool for exploration—is just a mistake. Not only does nature not care about our choice of the "best" method, but it reminds us how arrogant we continue to be as a species. It's like we haven't learned anything from our past errors.

If you pay attention to the sciences, you will notice that today everything is termed "science," because it's cool and it gets funded. Starting with physics, the most basic and scientific of the sciences, the concept of science expanded into chemistry and biology, the basic sciences, then branched out to the human sciences, including medicine and health sciences, then to more subjective disciplines such as economics and psychology. Today we even have a political "science", and while I'd love to, I've never seen a politician being studied in a lab. Academics has only stopped short of proclaiming a "divinity science" (as far as I know). Every academic wants their field to be relevant and to carry authority, to be "scientific" (again, there's that need for external validation), but the truth is that all of these sciences are not the same, other than the fact that people keep publishing peer-reviewed papers in each field and agreeing to agree that they're doing science.

The funny thing about all those sciences is that the more the discipline is related to humans, the less "scientific," or exact and objective, it gets. We are taught to believe that the world is exact and deterministic, that it is only our lack of knowledge about all the variables in a given system that prevents us from fully understanding and predicting its behavior. (To be fair, quantum mechanics has broken that paradigm and shown us that the world is not really deterministic, but most scientists would still say that the impact of that paradigm shift is on a very small scale [in the subatomic world] and thus does not influence our lives.) But for anyone paying attention, that's not what life shows.

What we can notice just by observing is that once we've incorporated the human element into a field of study, we simply can't have access to all variables anymore. Not because we don't yet have the technology to access all variables, but because those variables do not exist deterministically when dealing with human beings. This is because humans are conscious beings, and consciousness interacts with space-time but it doesn't *belong* in space-time.

Let that sink in for a while. The human element introduces variables that can't be accounted for. It is not by chance that my professors at medical school used to say, "Medicine is a combination of science and art." For all our scientific advancement, that's still true. Take the placebo effect, for example—the phenomenon by which patients appear to cure themselves simply by believing a treatment works. We don't fully understand how the placebo effect operates, but studies have shown that simply emulating a treatment (like taking a pill the patient *knows* to be a placebo) still improves clinical response. This is a good example of how consciousness creates third-person reality. The placebo has zero effect in the mechanics of 3D, but the action taken by the patient in their first-person consciousness space is enough to create a change in how they perceive the reality of the disease. The placebo effect tends to be more pronounced in more subjective medical conditions (like pain, stress, and fatigue), perhaps because the reality-creating power of consciousness is easier to notice in subjective experience, but there are countless reports of people who have been cured from pretty serious and readily quantifiable diseases as well. As my professors used to say, medicine is not pure science. And that's a good thing.

As a matter of fact, not even physics, our most "scientific" science, is immune to consciousness. Although physicists have been avoiding the question for a hundred years now, there's clearly something going on with consciousness and the collapse of the wave function—a phenomenon of quantum mechanics that seems to be triggered by consciousness. The general idea is that certain measurements in the microscopic world don't have a defined value until a conscious being goes there and takes the measurement. Prior to that, the measurement is a cloud of potentialities, every time showing a different result. I'm not a physicist and I won't venture into that space, but it strikes me that our most scientifically advanced machines today, quantum computers, have had as their greatest feat the generation of true random numbers. Classic computers, you see, can't generate true random numbers. When you use the RAND() function in Excel, that number isn't random at all, and its generation is completely deterministic. It's just the program tricking you into believing that it's created something out of nothing.

Amazingly enough, however, quantum computers are able to generate true random numbers, because the underlying technology uses a property of nature that is truly randomic. And that came from a scientific revolution that has been going on for over a hundred years already (quantum mechanics). Like classic computers, human beings are not that great at generating true random numbers (probably because of memory and ingrained behavioral patterns in the brain), but humans are definitely capable of creative work. Creating something out of nothing is our thing. Is that thing coming from a brain that doesn't generate random numbers very well, or does it come from consciousness? Could it be the case that every creation is some sort of channeling from first-person reality to third-person reality? And now we're creating AI machines that apparently do similar creative work (thus the question of whether those machines are as conscious as we). While I hope quantum mechanics and the AI revolution will prove somehow to have been an evolutionary step toward a true science of consciousness, I wonder how many future revolutions in physics and how many more centuries we'll need to fully evolve from mere random number generation to a complete understanding of the experiential nature of the universe.

That's time we don't have. To heal our world today and evolve from monkeys with nuclear weapons to something better, we need to start understanding spirituality *now*.

9. Basic Concepts

OK, now that we've gotten some distance from the old ways of seeing the world and the sciences, and you know that there are very strict limits to how traditional science can inform us on the spiritual realm, it is time to make another decision:

1. You can stop reading this book, because from now on we will be letting go of all classic scientific thinking (but not of rationality). Or...
2. You can open your mind and learn what has been shown by human beings that claim to directly connect with the spiritual realm. These are channelers, intuitives, and others who claim to have had extrasensorial conscious experiences (that is, conscious/qualia experiences that are not related to information obtained via the five senses). Near-death experiences (NDEs) are a good example of ordinary people going through extraordinary sensorial conscious experiences.

I know. How can we know there's any validity to the idea of direct connection to the spiritual realm? From a scientific perspective, we can't. That was the whole idea behind part 1 of this book. From now on, the method is different. The way I see it, there are three different approaches to exploring the first-person realm of reality:

1. One is by listening to as many channelers, intuitives, and other experiencers as possible, so you can try to capture a core message that is common to all or most of them.
2. Another is by looking inside and using your own feelings (your own consciousness or your own internal compass) to validate or refute the information. If it resonates with you and it works in your life, who cares if it's real in third-person reality? It is real for you!
3. Finally, by using your own conscious exploration via meditation, contemplation, and other methods. It might be hard to believe for the uninitiated, but it's amazing how new and impossible synchronicities and personal experiences will start coming to you once you open yourself to them.

Remember, the value is in the message, not in the messenger. It doesn't matter where the message comes from as long as it resonates with you. This is not traditional science anymore. Spiritual insights often come from those who haven't formally studied the topic, who are just relaying what they experience and feel. We may tend to think that less informed people would be more susceptible to imagination or making up stories. While that might be true, couldn't the opposite also be true?

Couldn't overeducation hinder a connection with subtle conscious experiences, intuitions, and inspirations?

The spiritual concepts and ideas in the sections that follow were obtained through these three methods from a variety of sources (the Acknowledgments section at the beginning of this book gives a small sample). Part 2 of this book summarizes these ideas, which I have absorbed and collected for many years through channeling sessions, videos, testimonies of all kinds, NDE stories, books, and open-minded scientific discussions. All of these ideas have been validated (for what it's worth and for my own purposes) by my inner self and through my own exploration as well. This validation suffices for me, but you should seek your own validation by using the same methods.

The need for us to start understanding and exploring the dual nature of reality is pressing. There's too much at stake for us to stay so attached to the old ways. If we don't do anything about it, we'll continue to live in eternal ignorance, which is not going to be eternal bliss.

This second part of the book is less original than parts 1 and 3, because these ideas have been reframed over and over again through various philosophies and religious or spiritual schools of thought. What I aim to do here is introduce old ideas to people who need a fresh reboot of their spiritual journey. Because the whole point of this book is that consciousness is real and should be taken seriously even by those people who are rational and can't believe in anything. Part 2 is an attempt at deriving or at least reinterpreting certain spiritual ideas from the perspective of consciousness and first-person reality. There are many spiritual frameworks and prisms you can use to develop ideas similar to those that follow, but having a framework like the first-/third-person reality model might be a little more palatable for those more rationally inclined.

You Exist

I first heard this idea, in this form, from the nonphysical being Bashar, speaking through the medium Darryl Anka. *You exist.* It's so simple and obvious, yet it isn't.

We've heard this before. It's similar to the maxim "Know Thyself" or Descartes's *Cogito, ergo sum* ("I think, therefore I am"). Now, I'm no philosopher, and this is not a philosophy book. It is (I hope) a short, pragmatic initiation guide into spirituality. So, for our purposes, "you exist" means that... you exist! Yay!

Seriously, now, the meaning is deep. It means your existence is *fundamental*. Not in the sense that other people can't live without you, but in the sense that your existence is necessary before anything else can take place. It comes before anything else, before all matter, before the planets and the known universe, even before time itself (and space-time). It means you've always existed and you will always exist. It means you can't be destroyed. It means you can't die. It means that everything else that exists came after you and from you. *It actually means you are God.*

God may be a loaded word and can create unease for those more rational and less religious. Conversely, the idea that *we* are God can be difficult to swallow for those who are religious and see themselves as *created beings* who are *separated* from God. (The idea of *separation* is further explored in part 3 of this book and is at the root of most problems we face as humanity.) Spiritual people like to use other names, like *Source.* More technically, God can be understood as *consciousness*, and for this discussion, we're going to leave it at that and not try to understand God descriptively. As I've said earlier, consciousness is *fundamental* (in the same way that God is considered to be fundamental), so it cannot be divided. Something *fundamental*, by definition, cannot be split into two or more parts; if it could, the parts would then be fundamental. Therefore, we as consciousness cannot be *a part* of God. Although our physical bodies could be understood as a creation by consciousness (or God), at the consciousness level, we are *one with God.*

Just like pain, God is something that needs to be *experienced.* It can be seen as pure qualia and pure experience, a sort of pure consciousness or *Source Consciousness.* Here, I'm not referring to my individual experience of consciousness or yours, but to the more abstract idea of consciousness as a (nonmeasurable and noncomputable) space or "force field" that is capable of creating and experiencing physical realities. It's like God is a living blank canvas that can paint its own pictures. And that's pretty much what people mean when they say that God is love, because love is pure qualia. Love is a driving force, because everything that exists physically would have originated from first-person reality, where God/Source/consciousness is all there is.

You exist means *you are God.* Let that sink in for a long while. This is of utmost importance. It's not an idea that you acknowledge intellectually and then move on to the next page. It is the most profound thing you could ever be told. It's an idea of tremendous consequence. Because when you truly and fully internalize this idea, you do become God. *In practice and for real.*

For example, when you know you exist, you're no longer afraid of dying, because you cannot not exist. Isn't it a godlike thing, not being afraid of dying? Or of anything at all? All of a sudden, you can completely trust life, because you know there is absolutely nothing anyone can do to cause you harm. You know that even if someone kills you, you still can't be hurt. If you can't feel this in your core, you haven't yet understood *you exist.* And that's OK. I told you it wasn't simple. Yet, it is completely possible. Many people have achieved that understanding and that state of peace.

You exist beats all other spiritual concepts and ideas. And that's why it was the first one I introduced to you. If you can grasp *you exist*, you have it all. That's all you need.

It is important to understand that *you exist* is not by any means an arrogant idea. The acknowledgment that you are God means that you are a piece of God. Not in a quantitative sense, as discussed earlier, but a manifestation of God just like everything else that exists (at least, everything that exists in first-person reality). *You exist* informs you that all of your fellow human beings and all other animals and sentient beings—those that show correlates of pain, for example—are also pieces of God, and have the same attributes and powers as God. In other words, we are God (some like to say *the universe*) experiencing itself.

To make more sense of the idea of being a *piece* of God while neither you as consciousness nor God can be measured or divided, think of *infinity*. Within an inch of a ruler, there are infinite points. If God is an infinite ruler, then each individualized consciousness can be understood as an inch with infinite points within an infinite ruler. Just as we have infinities that are bigger than others, we can also have indivisible consciousnesses that are part of an even "bigger" indivisible consciousness. We are one with God just like an infinite inch is one with an infinite ruler.

You exist also informs you that this life on Earth is just an experience and not your real state of being. You are not a by-product of your brain. You are *fundamental*. The brain comes after you and is your own godlike creation. The brain and all matter are creations of a consciousness that allows them to live a human experience (or a dolphin experience or a tree experience or, who knows, even a rock experience).

When I had the NDE described in chapter 7, I wasn't Daniel anymore. I didn't have an identity. I couldn't feel emotions or have any sensations. The only feeling was pure peace. There was nothing to interact with. Nothing but myself. I was a monad, a single unit, floating in the void. *I simply existed. And it felt good.*

Oneness

Oneness is the idea that all is one and one is all. This idea is found in the channeled communications known as the Ra Material, as well as Aaron Abke's *Law of One* YouTube series. In a sense, the concept derives from *you exist*. If we are all of the same conscious nature, then we are all one and the same. In a sense, oneness is not necessarily a spiritual idea. If you think we are all members of just one humanity and just one planet, you already have a sense of what it means.

Yet, this is one of the ideas we need the most as humans living on a planet that is only getting smaller and smaller for all of us. It is one of the most pragmatic spiritual ideas, because it essentially tells you that when you hurt someone, you're hurting yourself. You're hurting the collective. It's an old idea.

Despite the idea being old and kind of obvious, we're still extremely individualistic. We just can't always see ourselves in others. It is only when you really embrace the idea from a spiritual perspective that it starts to have some effect. From a true oneness perspective, when you hurt someone, you're not just hurting the collective. In actuality, lots of people couldn't care less about the collective. When you fully internalize the idea of oneness, you start noticing that when you hurt someone else, you are really hurting yourself. You can feel it. In first-person reality, all is *energy* and *vibration*. (I won't try to define the meaning of these words in the context of spirituality, but they convey the idea of the spiritual relationship between things or a state of being.) Hurting others brings your own vibration down, likely even more than that of the person being hurt. Hurting others hurts you, too. Directly and immediately.

The good news is that the same logic works the other way as well. When you love others, you also feel loved. Eventually, you begin to realize that all is one, one is love, and all is love. Love is the force, in first-person reality physics, that builds realities. Your life is a construct of your love. And your love helps build other people's realities as well, for you are already one with them, collaborating with them from consciousness space.

Ultimately, you realize that you are a source of love. When you love someone, that whole energy exists inside of you. The energy is you. It is by loving others that you build love in yourself. That's how you *become love*. You learn that you don't necessarily need to be loved by others. You can completely fulfill your demand for love by just building it in yourself and channeling it onto others. Because others are you. We are all one and the same.

If we truly understood and embraced oneness, we'd never ever be waging wars. The very thought of it would never cross our minds. When we understand who we really are and who others really are, which is one and the same, the ideas of resistance, defiance, and war simply wouldn't make sense. They would just feel plainly and completely absurd. I wish we had a technology that could easily show how everything is connected and how whatever we do to others we automatically do to ourselves. How building a world without war starts with not accepting conflicts anymore in our own individual lives.

Understanding oneness is letting go of fear. It is letting go of lack and absence. It is knowing you are one with everything that exists and you'll always have everything you need, because nothing you need is outside of you.

What You *Feel* Is What You Get

You've probably already used or heard the expression "What you see is what you get" (or WYSIWYG). The spiritual version of it is "What you feel is what you get." Another way to put it would be "What you put out is what you get back." The most popular name for it is the *law of attraction*, popularized most recently by the nonphysical entities known as Abraham, via the medium Esther Hicks.

The general understanding of the concept is very much related to the idea of karma: whatever you do, good or bad, will return to you. The original idea is quite mechanistic, and it was probably presented that way because it makes it easier to understand by those whose rationality is firmly embedded in the mechanics of matter and third-person reality.

From a first-person-reality perspective, though, once you've mastered the concepts of consciousness and oneness, the interpretation of the law of attraction becomes much simpler. The idea then becomes "Whatever you vibrate is that which you feel." As we discussed earlier, you don't need to *do* good to *receive* good back. When you *vibrate* good, you automatically *feel* good. It's nothing that went out and came back. We're all one. There's no outside or inside of one. There's just oneness.

The challenge, therefore, is to bring our individual selves (which are little pieces of the whole) to a state of being that feels good, that is joyful and uplifting. And this has everything to do with focus and attention. You are the result of your choices. Your choices are a result of your beliefs. Your beliefs are a result of where you put your focus and attention. Whatever you dedicate your attention to becomes part of you, which is why it is so critical for you to filter what you consume, from food to TV shows to the people you interact with. *Whatever you decide to believe becomes your reality.* This is so important. You know when someone confidently says, "I got this!" and they indeed get it done? That go-get-it attitude is a typical example of how your belief shapes your reality. And your beliefs are always yours to choose.

Do you see? It's all you. *It has always been all you.* You are the master of your reality and your first-person experience of the world. It is you who decides what you let in, meaning that you decide, by directing your focus, what you vibrate and resonate with. If your focus is on uplifting things and thoughts, your experienced reality will be uplifting as well. What you get is what you feel. If you want to be happy, you need to build happiness. You are a creator! If you want to be loved, you need to build love within, which means vibrating with the love energy that is always available in consciousness space for you to tune in with. It's like a radio. You have to tune in to the frequency of that which you want to feel. And when you find that frequency (which might take time, focus, and dedication), you can feel it. And what you feel becomes what you get.

The element of attraction is a more relatable way to interpret the concept, but on a more subtle level, this is what's happening: you become the energy that you build inside of yourself by resonating with the energies that already exist in consciousness space. All spiritual energy and every vibration you're capable of feeling exists in consciousness space. It is up to you to choose which parts of the energy spectrum you're going to resonate with. You don't really "attract" it from somewhere else. You just tune in and become one with it. It all takes place within your own first-person reality.

Everything Is Here and Now

If consciousness and first-person reality are more fundamental than space-time, then space and time don't actually exist, at least not fundamentally; they're more like constructs within consciousness. And if there is no space and time, everything is, by consequence, here and now. As a scientist, I find this mind-boggling. Because, in 3D (that is, in our physical, three-dimensional world), we clearly have a timeline. This is so ingrained in our physical minds, in our brains, that even many spiritual schools of thought adopt timeline perspectives. For example, a spiritual belief in reincarnation will usually assume that those many lives have happened in temporal sequence.

Communications by many of the most "modern" (more recently channeled) spiritual entities, however, speaking through completely different people, inform us that all those life experiences happen at the "same time"—at least, from your higher consciousness's first-person perspective. Not only that, they claim that we never really leave that realm, the spiritual location, to exist in this third-person reality location, because the concept of location does not apply in consciousness. The puppeteer is always there and has always been there in consciousness. The puppeteer *exists*. So, it is not like we keep coming and going perpetually along many sequential lives. Everything is happening or has already happened or will still happen in the *here and now*.

I find *everything is here and now* the most challenging spiritual concept for the human brain to master. My feeling is that one would need to be quite bent into first-person reality to make sense of it. When I had my NDE, I didn't have a sense of time. I was at a standstill. Many reports of several kinds of spiritual experiences also reveal this dissociation from time. Sometimes people go on entire astral journeys, vivid in detail and moments, only to find out that physical time has elapsed at a completely different rate.

The idea that we are spiritual beings living one or many physical experiences without ever leaving the spiritual realm is an interesting one. Our true spiritual self is the puppeteer, while our multiple physical egos and identities living amazing human life experiences across time are our puppets, the puppets of our true self. This concept is difficult for the human mind to grasp because it creates another perceived duality: the spir*iduality* of the puppet and the puppeteer. Essentially, it is the same first- and third-person duality of reality that we discussed in chapter 5. The puppeteer is that version of us living in first-person reality while the puppets are us living in third-person reality.

It feels confusing, but it need not be. It is confusing because if we exist in this moment as pure consciousness (the puppeteer), then why do we only have access to the conscious experience of the puppet? In other words, why can't we remember or why can't we connect with the experiences of the other puppets, who are living other lives in this exact moment in consciousness? Could that be the role of our brains? Would our brains' job be to *filter* the puppet/puppeteer interface in such a way that the puppeteer can fully experience all puppets at once while each puppet can only experience itself? Could that brain filter, if it exists, be bypassed? It turns out that many spiritual people claim to connect with their other selves (the other puppets). As a matter of fact, many channelers claim to be channeling their own selves from other physical lives!

It is hard to tell what is going on behind the scenes. But it makes sense, if consciousness exists outside of space-time, that spiritual experiences would be poorly recollected and understood from a time and space perspective. Our physical brains were not selected to make sense of that kind of experience. Yet, we have this dissociation of time in our own lives in 3D. Do something enjoyable, and it feels like time flies. Do something painful, and it feels like it takes forever. And we do go through lots and lots of painful moments in 3D reality.

That's when the *everything is here and now* concept becomes more actionable. The best way to dissociate and separate from the chain of events that gives us the perception of time and populates our physical minds is to meditate. Meditation is a technique for quieting the brain by focusing on breathing. As we take the brain out of the equation through meditation, we bring ourselves to that timeless and spaceless state, which enhances the puppet's resonance with the puppeteer, the true self. By meditating, we better connect with our higher selves (the part of our consciousness that lives outside space-time). We get in closer touch with the feeling that, at any time, all is well. *All is always well.* The human experience is just that, an experience. And our true self lives in peace in consciousness space. All we need to do, every once in a while, to remind ourselves of that is take some deep breaths, relax, and reconnect with that deeper reality.

Just like any other exploration or learning curve in life, developing proficiency in meditation may take time and dedication. But life is always about the path, not the destination. Just get started with it and enjoy the ride. If there is no time, there is no hurry.

Wanting

One of the main challenges I observe in people who try to become more spiritual is that despite all efforts, they still don't get what they want, whether it's material possessions, love, relationships, or something else. This may sound like a bummer, but spirituality is not really about getting what you want—or rather, not necessarily so. Spirituality is more akin to *being* what you want. And you don't really need any spiritual knowledge in order to *be* what you want. That's already what each one of us is doing right now, automatically, in the sense that we are always getting that which we *are*. We are what we vibrate with. We are what we feel inside. If we feel happy, we are happy and we get happiness. If we feel lacking, we are in lack and we get less and less. If we feel abundant, we are abundant and we get more and more.

People tend to believe that what they feel depends on what happens to them in third-person reality. "I'm sad because of what they did to me." Nothing could be further from the truth! You are sad because you chose to be sad, because you allowed others or your circumstances to make you feel sad. So, do you get more and more of what you want? Not necessarily. You get more and more of what you *allow*!

As we've already discussed, everything derives from you, your beliefs, and your choices. You get what you choose to feel—the energies you choose to vibrate with and focus on—and what you feel is who you become. *Know thyself,* remember? Third-person reality doesn't make you; it is *you* who create third-person reality.

That said, spirituality can help you get what you want, because your wants also come from who you are. Wanting is similar to will. The difference is that *wanting* is usually a lower-frequency feeling more associated with third-person validation and metrics. *Will*, on the other hand, comes from your higher self. That's why we talk of *free will* but not *free wanting*. If you can tell and feel the difference between the two concepts, it'd be more advisable for you to focus on your *will* than on your *wants*, since a strong *will* automatically creates all of the little parts (the wants) to get itself fulfilled.

You still can get what you want, of course. We do it all the time with different degrees of success. The more aligned your *wants* with your *will*, the greater the success. Getting what you want is thus all about working on who you are and building the character you want to play on this stage, which is your life in 3D. But you need to choose wisely, because you'll be getting lots and lots of that which you become. The process of getting what you want involves turning yourself into that person who would naturally have whatever it is that you want. Even if what you want is something very specific (like a certain house, for example), the way to get it is by focusing on seeing yourself living in that house and *feeling* the emotions you expect to feel when you do occupy the house. By living the emotions of a certain situation in your "head" (i.e., in first-person reality), you manifest that same emotion and experience (i.e., the same qualia) in third-person reality.

It's not actually about the thing you want. It is much more about living the conscious experience of interacting in 3D with that which you want by *feeling* the energy of that experience. You may not necessarily get the very house you were hoping for, but you are going to get something that vibrates in the same energy you first used to create that reality within you. *Your reality is your own creation.* Getting what you want is much more related to transforming yourself from the inside, hopefully by *improving* yourself and your character on the stage and letting the mechanics of life take care of the rest. You might find that by doing so, your wants actually change as well, and you end up getting much more and better things or situations or experiences than what you originally expected.

Even though you can do this and totally succeed at it, focusing on having objects and things means attaching more value to things than they actually deserve. Things are just things. What really matters to you are the *emotions and feelings* associated with interacting with that thing. That is, what matters is the *experience*. And you don't even need the "thing" to build those emotions and feelings within you. The "thing" is more like an amulet you believe you need to have to experience what you want to experience. You are so much bigger than whatever thing you can think of. See yourself as big; see things as small. When you do that, getting things will be easier, and you'll also realize they were not all that important in the first place. Don't *need* things and don't obsess about having them. *Needing* is trapping energy. It keeps you in the state of needing. *Wanting* without *needing* is more effective in helping you get what you want.

When you badly want something and you *need* it, you can create an obsession. Obsession can indeed bring you a whole lot, but it comes with its own energy. And other things that come with it (the need for your success to be validated by others, for example) may not put you in a good place. Many people, because they are so immersed in third-person reality and its metrics, only care about succeeding in those metrics, and they'll obsess about that. There is no right or wrong energy; it all exists for you to make use of. You can pick an obsessive energy to resonate with, if you like. Many of the most successful people (by 3D metrics) succeed by making use of that kind of energy. But uplifting energies will create a more uplifting life experience for you (naturally), even if they won't necessarily help you with the metrics. This is one of those choices that come with spiri*duality*: you can choose to build a successful life for yourself to enjoy or one for others to admire and measure. By focusing on metrics, you can actually limit yourself and fall behind your full potential for realization. Because love, which is the creative energy that creates realities, has no measure.

The thing to remember is that the process of becoming who you want to be always starts with an *emotion* (excitement, obsession, happiness, wanting, etc.). Emotion is the reality-creating driving force. You need to build that emotion and the *will* first within yourself (in first-person reality) before you can see that situation manifest in third-person reality. Third-person reality is just a consequence. It is a mirror of what happens in first-person reality, both individually and collectively. If you use an uplifting emotion, that's the nature of the experiences you're going to get. The same goes for any other emotion you choose to vibrate with. Whatever you vibrate with will manifest in your third-person reality. This is continuously happening, all the time. That's why choosing wisely and focusing on the set of emotions you want to nurture is so critical for manifesting whatever you want to have in your life.

Then why is it that what I want takes time or doesn't happen at all? you may ask. Because you don't *become* the vibration by simply choosing to vibrate. Choosing is the first step, and it's a critical one. But you need to *become* that vibration by keeping your focus throughout the continued iterations and challenges that 3D will continue to throw at you. You also need to *overcome the fear* of not getting or achieving what you want. Because fear is just another emotion. It builds a reality around exactly what you're fearing. Let go of all fear. Don't put yourself in a state of *needing* what you want, because needing what you don't have is also an emotion that only brings you more needing (*needing* is a form of fear and a form of *not having*).

You want to use the right emotion, a positive emotion associated with all the excitement of *knowing* you already have what you want. In first-person reality, build the feeling that you already have it. That's the emotion you want. Then, for you to manifest that in 3D, the process may take more or less time depending on the initial gap between where you are and where you want to be and the number of iterations required for your conscious intent to manifest that in 3D. Because 3D has its rules (the laws of physics, for example) and you are always cocreating 3D reality with other consciousnesses as well (your fellow human beings). Just remember: build the reality you want within yourself first and you won't need 3D to manifest it as much anymore, even if it will.

All Is Always Well

There are countless NDE accounts of people who have gone through death and returned to tell their stories. One recurrent aspect of the story is that people feel indifferent to their bodies or lives on Earth when they see them from that other realm. From that space, they know this life on Earth is just an experience. And they know that all is always well, no matter what.

All is always well. That's all you need to know. Whatever the problem seems to be here in 3D, there's nothing that can harm you, remember? You are a piece of Source Consciousness. Indestructible. Just focus on your energy. Find your excitement. And trust life to dissipate any problems you appear to be having. Problems are a matter of interpretation. As the saying goes, you can see the glass as half-empty or half-full. It is your inner vibration that makes the choice to interpret your reality as being one or the other.

Problems will always come and always go. The only possible way to feel that flow is in time, and time only exists in third-person reality. Whenever third-person reality becomes too much to handle, just turn inside, back to first-person reality. It may take time (from a third-person-reality perspective), but you'll always find within yourself everything you need to deal with any situation. The inspiration to find a solution that will take you out of any problem is always there in consciousness space for you to reach out to. All you need to do is search for it. You can always connect with that higher part of yourself that sees everything from an outside perspective. Ask your higher self for help and listen for the inspiration that will come to you. And just know that no matter what happens, *all is always well.*

Problems

You don't need to spend too much time with human beings to notice something that is practically fundamental to human existence: *problems*. Absolutely everyone seems to have problems. Problems are at the very core of the human experience on Earth. It is really difficult to not have problems around here. When people find themselves without a problem, they'll be sure to create one. Because not having a problem is also seen as a problem. People love problems. They just can't live without them.

There are two important things for you to learn about problems:

1. There's absolutely no problem that can't be immediately eliminated from your life with a little reframing.
2. Never fall victim to your problems.

Let's start with #1. The thing about problems is that they're all in you. No, I don't mean that *you* are the problem—although you could be! What I'm saying is that third-person reality has no problems. Actually, third-person reality is a pretty empty space. There are no feelings in third-person reality, only objects moving about and bumping into each other according to the laws of physics. Problems only exist in first-person reality, because a problem is that which you *feel* to be a problem.

We actually need to define *problem*, because a single situation can always be seen as a *problem* but it can also be seen as a *challenge* or *opportunity*, no matter what it is. Even if you perceive it as the end of your life or the end of the world, it can always be reframed and seen as an opportunity—to learn, to grow, to move on. Or, of course, you can choose to see it as a problem. So, a problem is simply a situation that you have *decided to interpret* as a problem—that is, a situation regarded as unwelcome or harmful that needs to be dealt with and overcome.

But spirituality is not about faith; it is about choice. You can choose to believe you have a *problem* and you need God to help and solve it or you can choose to believe you have an *opportunity*. You don't need to take God out of the equation. You can actually *thank* God for giving you the opportunity to learn and grow through that situation that seems to be a problem. And there's nothing wrong with asking for help, from God or whomever. It is just nicer to ask for help to overcome a challenge and explore an opportunity than to ask for help solving a problem. Because problems suck! Nobody wants to deal with problems. But we all like to engage with challenges and opportunities.

This problem vs. challenge thing may seem like just semantics, but it's not. It's not all the same thing. The story you tell yourself about the events in your life makes the entire difference. Tell yourself you have a problem and you've got yourself a problem. You've become a victim to your own creation, which is the second important thing to learn about problems: *nothing positive comes from seeing yourself as a victim*. In fact, if you believe you are a victim, the universe will be sure to confirm your idea. You have that much power.

The universe is weird and funny. It will believe whatever you tell it. Tell it you are a victim and just observe the process that unfolds in front of your own eyes as everyone else starts believing you are a victim too! This happens because we are all one in consciousness. What you believe about yourself you automatically communicate to others via consciousness space. Some will try to help you, some will tell you to stop being a victim, but nothing can be better for you than not being a victim in the first place. And that's your own choice to make. Nobody can make that decision for you. Victims are hopeless and helpless. There's nothing anyone can really do for them. The first thing you need (so help from others will be effective for you) is to stop believing you're a victim. You'll be much better off, and much more "helpable," if you choose to believe you already have everything you need to overcome any obstacles. You have the power to summon all the resources you need to overcome anything; help from others is just one of them.

Now, tell yourself and tell the universe you have an opportunity, and you've got yourself an opportunity! It's as simple as that. It is all about what you tell yourself. Telling yourself you have an opportunity, at minimum, puts you in a place of hope and pursuit, which is a positive and expansive energy. Conversely, dealing with situations as problems only brings negativity to your life.

You can use the concepts described in this book to help you deal with any kind of problem. *You exist!* Even if you die, you still don't have a problem. You just move on to the next phase of the game. At any time, *all is well.* Third-person reality is a stage, and you are the actor. No matter what happens to the character, the actor is always fine. Reframe every one of your problems and choose to live a problem-free life. It's completely within reach. You only need to do the work. Start with little problems. See them for what they are: *little* problems. Then, keep expanding the concept to bigger and bigger problems until you reach the point where you have no problems at all in your life. Remember, you are an infinite being, and no problem can be as infinite as you.

Justice and Empathy

Justice is a concept very much entwined with problems. A lot of what we see as problematic in our lives is related to what we consider injustice. As humans, we believe in all sorts of injustices, from social injustice to things that happen to us undeservedly to believing God has been unfair to us. Invariably, we eventually find ourselves victims of others or of our circumstances. The idea of injustice is also a primary motivator for war and other kinds of social unrest. Almost every form of unrest starts with someone exploiting some sort of injustice suffered by an individual who is representative of a determined group.

The thing about injustice that makes it so tricky to deal with is that it doesn't exist in physical reality, so it cannot be measured. Injustice, like pain, only exists in consciousness. Because injustice is not a fact; it is a *perception*, another type of qualia. If someone steals my bicycle and I don't consider that just, that comes not from the fact that the bicycle was stolen but from the *sentiment*

I experienced having my bicycle stolen. Had I had no sentiment, there would be no injustice. That sentiment doesn't take place in third-person reality, yet it causes all sorts of consequences in physical reality, from fights to lawsuits to wars.

If justice takes place in first-person reality, then it's governed by spiritual "laws." We tend to believe that justice is accomplished in 3D, but what happens in 3D is simply an *illusion* of justice. If someone kills your loved one, for example, and justice determines that they be killed as well, was justice achieved? You might feel vindicated, but no justice was really carried out. Your loved one isn't back. Maybe you believe your pain was transferred to the perpetrator, but was it? How can you know?

The idea of justice exists in the universe, but it's different than we think. If one is all and all is one, how can there be injustice in the first place? At any time, everything is well. If that is so, there can't be injustice.

What you vibrate with is what you feel. If you don't vibrate with injustice, you won't feel injustice. The perception of injustice only comes from *separation* (from Source) and individualization. You need polarization between two parts for injustice to occur. Yes, we experience the feeling of injustice, because the framework through which society chooses to interpret reality allows for the idea of injustice. By that interpretation, if there's injustice in the world, then somebody needs to rectify it and bring justice to it. We only need justice because we've created the idea of injustice in the first place. But that's our own creation. Fundamentally, the universe is just.

The idea of injustice also exists because of our capacity for feeling empathy, another type of qualia that only takes place in first-person reality. We can only feel the injustices suffered by others either because we have experienced similar feelings in similar situations or because we're capable of imagining what it feels like to be in that situation. One way or another, the whole concept of injustice only happens in first-person reality.

Remember, first-person reality cannot be measured. Therefore, dealing with justice and injustice is one of the most fruitless endeavors of humankind. We make use of tribunals and juries and verdicts and wars and redistribution of assets and all sorts of third-person-reality manipulations to try and achieve a balance of first-person reality. But we never achieve that, because first-person reality is fluid and ethereal, not mechanical. The pain you suffered from an "injustice" has already been felt; it can't really be repaired.

Nevertheless, we're always engaging in all sorts of conflicts to bring about justice. It is interesting to notice how much effort and energy we put as humans into justice-making. It is a constant struggle. More interesting still is that most of us won't notice how engaging with injustice can actually potentialize it. In 3D, you might even see results from trying to create justice. In first-person reality, however, you become closer and closer to what you oppose. The more you oppose something or someone, the more that entity becomes part of your mental universe, and the more you spend your time and your life with that entity and the conflict around it. If you obsess enough about the conflict, your life becomes it. Instead of getting rid of what you oppose and what doesn't serve you, you essentially become part of it.

When it comes to the spirituality of justice, the great news is that all you consider just or unjust happens only within you. It is all your *perception*, and because it is a perception that exists within you, you always have the power to reframe and dissipate that pain. Regardless of what others have done to you, you can always choose not to be a victim of injustice. Even if you *are* a victim (by 3D metrics), you can still choose to not *feel* like one. And that makes the entire difference in how you live and perceive your life.

Many would disagree with that idea. People often resort to the idea of vengeance as a means to alleviate pain, for example. Because we're empathic beings, we believe that we can have our pain rectified by causing the same pain to our offenders. That idea is fallacious at several levels.

First, nobody has the power to cause you pain. I know this might be difficult to swallow, but it is what it is. No matter what others do to you, the pain only happens within you; therefore, it is only there if you allow it to be there. It may take time and practice for anyone to learn how to modulate pain internally, but it's entirely possible.

Remember, whatever happens, you can always reframe and reinterpret.

Every loss is a learning experience. Many people have already learned the power of thankfulness, but most people do only thank for the good things. Throughout my journey, I've come to learn that it's more important to be thankful for the bad and painful things than to be thankful for the good things. For it is the pain that helps you grow in consciousness. The good things are great to live and experience and we should all be thankful for those for sure, but they don't really force you to change and reinvent yourself. There's a lot of value and opportunity in pain if you decide to take advantage of it and use it to your benefit.

Likewise, if you try to inflict the same pain back onto the other person, you'll never be able to tell if you've achieved your goal. All you can do is assume they're in pain, but you won't know that for a fact. And even if they are in pain and you've succeeded at achieving that, they might have just been looking forward to experiencing that pain the entire time, in which case you've only done them a favor and there's no justice accomplished anyway. At the end of the day, we've all chosen, through our first-person reality intent, to be in this human form on this Earth and to go through the whole human experience—which at this stage of humanity includes all the pain that comes with it. No wonder feeling pain might be someone's goal, even if it is just the subconscious intent of their higher self. Because pain helps you grow. It's all part of our learning experience. Hopefully we'll one day grow as humanity to the point that we'll no longer need pain to get there.

Finally, the idea that retaliation can alleviate our pain is a fallacy because we're all one and the same. The pain you cause in others you're also causing to yourself. There is no vengeance. All vengeance you take is against yourself, even if you don't immediately notice it.

Empathy is a tool. Use it to bring good to your life. As much as you can and find reasonable, try to avoid using it to engage in conflicts of any kind. Use it to bring warmth to those who are cold. Don't use it to get cold, too. Always remember that the emotion you build up within yourself is the emotion that will permeate your life. Whatever you choose to build within becomes what you feel and who you are. If you choose well, that choice can make you *immune* to injustice. You'll never be a victim again.

Free Will

Free will is the last spiritual concept I'm going to discuss in part 2 of this little initiation book for rational people on the subject of spirituality. I left it for last because free will is, in my opinion, the most interesting concept to discuss with rational people, like scientists or business people. Also, the idea that we are free to make our own choices is one of the most repeated and universally known spiritual principles. Historically and religiously, this idea has been related to choices between right and wrong or good and evil. When Google decided to use "Don't Be Evil" as its motto (later replaced by Alphabet, Google's parent company, with "Do the Right Thing"), corporate leadership was probably assuming the motto was to be followed by people who had *free will.*

The concept is so prevalent that it might not sound spiritual to you at all, just another fact of life that is taken for granted. Yet, *free will* is a *deeply spiritual* concept. If you believed in free will before reading this book, you were already a believer in the spiritual realm and first-person realities. And you didn't even know it!

Science does not acknowledge free will, first because it is technically poorly defined: Free of what, exactly? From a scientific perspective, our brains are incapable of making decisions free of external influence. All the brain ever does is process external information. A decision that is made free of external influence is one made not by the brain but by some other thing. Second, just as classical computers (based on classical physics) are not free to generate random numbers, classical brains (as scientists currently assume our brains to be) are equally unfree. Even if our brains were quantum-based, as some scientists of consciousness believe is the case (Roger Penrose and Stuart Hameroff come to mind), our decisions would not be free; they would be *random.* Can you imagine how crazier still this world would be if we made random decisions?

To be more precise, Penrose and Hameroff postulate that quantum effects in the brain are behind the phenomenon of *conscious experience*, not decision making. My understanding is that they consider our decisions to follow classical mechanics while the *conscious experience of knowing* which decision is made by the brain would be quantum in nature. Decisions made by the brain, according to our current science, follow a deterministic function. We may not know what a brain will eventually choose, for lack of knowledge of all the variables involved in information processing within that brain, but the idea is that we would know what the brain's decision would be if we had access to all the information. That's the modern assumption.

As a neuroscientist, I did not believe in *free will*. That actually felt freeing to me. Whatever I did and whatever I chose, it was not my fault or responsibility; *it was my brain's*. Not only that, the idea of the *absence of free will* is actually highly valuable in clinical practice. A patient who has a cerebral disorder cannot be held accountable for his actions, for he cannot totally control his brain. But do we even control our brains at all, dysfunctional or not? Or do brains control themselves? Have we found another spiri*duality*? Perhaps. The duality is still the same, just presenting in a different way.

In the case of *free will*, there is actually a semantic confusion that has developed over time. The confusion comes from associating *will* with either *decision* or *choice*. Those are very different concepts. A decision usually follows some sort of reasoning or algorithm. For example, a traffic light makes decisions nonstop. Now it's red; now it's green. You might argue that the decision was actually that of the engineer who designed the light, programming it to change color at intervals according to a timed system or information detected by sensors. But the engineer didn't make that decision creatively. She followed a certain rationale with the goal of optimizing traffic flow.

Most of our decisions are actually no-brainers (paradoxically, those are the decisions made by the brain). They just follow a predetermined and somewhat deterministic flow. When it comes to certain decisions, we don't even have a say. When you touch a hot plate and you immediately take your finger away, for example, that decision was not yours to make. The neurons in your spinal cord made the decision and took action for you, only letting you know about it after the fact. So, as you can see, there are many types of decisions.

Will is a different matter. Like pain, *will* doesn't exist in third-person reality. *Will* is a type of qualia; it is something you *feel*. Matter doesn't have *will*, no matter how well-organized it is. If it does, then it follows certain laws of nature that we are completely unaware of, laws whose understanding could reveal entire new realities to us (like consciousness and first-person realities). Could AI have *will*? What if we start perceiving a certain drive or determination in our AI models? Would that disprove the idea that matter cannot have *will*?

Well, not exactly. We already have that disproof, which is our own brain. If an AI starts showing *will*, it's probably because it's becoming like us, a little sentient. But that wouldn't mean that *will* is happening at the level of matter. Even if we could figure out how to set up an AI in such a way that it would demonstrate *will*, we probably would still not understand *why* or *how* that was happening. And we would remain completely at a loss to imagine what it would *feel like* to be an AI with *will*. Naturally, we'd humanize it and assume that its drive and determination felt to it just like ours feels to us, but there's no way we could prove that scientifically.

Just like science ignores the question of *why* the universe exists, it'd be happy enough to let go of the question of *why* an AI model claims to be conscious. Since it can't measure consciousness, science would gladly claim that it's just manifested behavior by the machine with no association with conscious experience (in other words, the AI would not be feeling anything). A certain scientist once said that *why* questions don't matter, that what matters are *what* and *how* questions, for those are the questions that allow us to build technology and gadgets (and nuclear weapons). I couldn't disagree more. *Why* questions are the most important of all. If anything, they serve to show us how limited we are, since we can't always answer them. That's plenty of value that those questions are giving us already. Instead of saying *why* questions don't matter, we should have the humility to accept that certain questions are not irrelevant or impossible, just beyond the scope of our favorite method, the scientific.

So, we have the concepts of *decision*, *will*, and *free*. *Decisions* are the result of cerebral activity. There are mechanics involved. *Will* happens in consciousness. And in the sense that it happens in consciousness, our *will* is indeed *free*. It is free of third-person realities, mechanics, and boundaries; it's actually more *fundamental*. It is *will* that is free to play with, and mess up in, third-person reality, not the other way around. If we choose to assume first-person reality to be indeed more fundamental than matter, *will* is the very thing that creates reality. In that sense, *will* would be related to and pretty much the same as *love*, a driving and creative force. Third-person reality exists, because that is the *will of Source Consciousness* (or God). And we are agents (sharing the same *nature*) of that Source, empowered with *will* just the same.

This duality remains at the intersection of both realms (first- and third-person realities). How is it that *will* interferes with the mechanics of decision-making? While that remains a mystery, I have a few ideas. First, *will* doesn't really interfere with decision-making at all. Decision-making may be deterministic (classical) or stochastic (quantum), but it's not *will*-driven. In other words, we don't have *free decision-making* as human beings. Our decision-making has pretty clear physical boundaries.

But we do have *free will*. And here is perhaps the most controversial sentence in the entire book: as conscious beings who build their own realities, we are free to *manifest* (i.e., bring into being) bodies and decision-making brains that were created by and serve a purpose to our higher selves. By evolving and improving who we are at our core, we manifest bodies and brains that operate according to that same energy. Our bodies and brains are always transforming to align with our state of being at the consciousness level. That's how our brains' decisions align with our *will*. Among other things, that may also be how the placebo effect operates: our *will* simply manifests a healthier body. No mechanics of third-person reality involved. A *free will* manifests third-person reality directly from the first-person realm.

The physical universe is contained in Source Consciousness, and the body is contained in its own square of consciousness space, which is controlled by the higher self. How exactly we are capable of changing our bodies and our third-person reality from first-person consciousness space, I can't tell. Could it be related to parallel realities in a multiverse, which would allow our consciousness to experience that version of 3D reality that better aligns with its will at each moment? I won't speculate further on any theories for the underlying mechanism of how the consciousness-matter interaction takes place. I will simply make the case for spiri*duality* again: the spiri*duality* of *creator* and *creation*.

By using *free will*, we can control our degree of *separation* from Source. In many different ways and forms at different moments of our lives, we can choose to understand ourselves more as *creator* or more as *creation*. The more *creation* we choose to see ourselves, the more at the mercy of third-person-reality mechanics we are, and the more physical and deterministic we feel the world around us to be. Also, the more hopeless we get, for we are just a creation. On the other hand, the more *creator* we choose to see ourselves, the more empowered we become with each and every aspect of our lives, including health and disease, relationships, and professional satisfaction. More than a tool we use to make every little decision in our daily lives, *free will* is the fine-tuning process that sets us more as *creation* or *creator*. And we have total control over this process from our first-person reality.

This is a good time to revisit our definition of spirituality: spirituality is a state of focusing on our reality as *creator*. The more spiritual people are, the less separated they perceive themselves to be from *Source* because they feel more as *one* with it. Less spiritual people tend to focus more on their reality as *creation*. There's nothing wrong with being in that state, but dwelling in a spiritual state gives you more control over your life. Your life becomes your creation, because you see yourself as a creator.

I have to be consistent with what I've been saying throughout the entire book: *consciousness is more fundamental than matter*. Either the brain is creating consciousness or consciousness is creating the brain. Regardless of which one is true, choosing to assume that consciousness is more fundamental naturally leads to a more spiritual life. I've made this choice, and I've built a more spiritual life for myself. And you can, too.

This whole idea that we exist in consciousness and are creators of realities may cause such an ontological shock in many readers that it's likely to be refuted outright. But causing an ontological shock, or at least opening you up to these ideas, is exactly the point of this book. I wouldn't be bothering to write this book if it wasn't something extremely important. There's an urgent need—and there are good theoretical and rational reasons—for us to question the current worldview of our civilization. That first-person reality is more fundamental is not a theory that can be proven by physics and science. It's a theory that can only be *felt* to make sense in consciousness. As such, it's not a theory to be imposed on others. It's a theory to be embraced only for those who *feel* that it will be helpful and uplifting and freeing for them to think in this new way.

After all, we all have *free will*.

10. Reshaping Your Life

This book is not a long introduction to spirituality, because the nature of the subject is actually quite simple. These ideas have been around forever. The challenge has always been to put them into practice. For a long time, humanity's lack of clarity came from a lack of scientific understanding about nature. Science took us out of the shadows and freed us, to a great extent, from misplaced beliefs and superstitions. But today the situation has reversed. We've become hostages of scientific reasoning, and we've lost touch with who we really are. Science has created great technology, but it hasn't made us better as people.

The goal of part 2 was not to unveil some incredible breakthrough in spirituality. There are many spiritual masters out there who do that job much better than I. Its intention was to build a bridge to help all those who find themselves hostages to the scientific and materialistic trap, allowing them to expand their worldview to include the spiritual aspect of things. The existence of a spiritual reality can be demonstrated by using the same first principles upon which science itself was founded. Just as believing in third-person reality was a *choice* that allowed for the emergence of science, we can make a better choice now, which is believing in first-person reality and opening a whole different set of possibilities for ourselves.

Science and spirituality are not mutually exclusive; they simply exist in different realms. And consciousness is the phenomenon that links those two realities. The idea of consciousness has been lost to us for ages, although it was hidden in plain sight the whole time. Now it's time to walk across that bridge. There's no reason the world should continue to dwell primarily in third-person reality, with scientific fact as the sole basis for its reasoning and policies. We are completely capable of finding balance between our inner and outer realities by promoting decision-making rationales that respect both worldviews. Eventually, I expect first-person reality to be shown to be more fundamental, but that really doesn't matter. What matters is that we can all live in peace in our spiri*duality*.

As you go through your life, do regularly revisit these ideas, particularly when you are going through pain and hardship. Take note of what resonates with you so you can easily find it again, should the need come. But the fact is, if you really internalize these ideas, it will be very hard for you to remain in any hardship. It's not that hardship will not come. In third-person reality, hardship is always being thrown at us. That's the whole point of third-person reality. It exists to challenge you and to allow you to explore the boundaries of existence. But if you manage to internalize the concepts presented in this book, hardship just won't feel as hard anymore. It will feel like a learning experience, an uplifting one. It won't be easy, and you won't be immune to every bad thing that might happen. But it is possible, and it can be very fulfilling.

Start by taking baby steps. *Trust* life while you apply the focus and energy needed to build the realities you want to experience. *Allow* the good and the bad things life will bring you throughout the process. Trust that life is constantly bringing you everything you need, even if you can't understand why or make sense of it. Allow the experience to unfold. Let all negative thoughts *dissipate* and dismiss all negative energy. One of the best ways to do this is by being thankful. Be thankful for everything that happens to you. Be thankful for the good things, for those are uplifting and joyful in nature. *But also be thankful for the difficult things, for those are the ones that will make you grow in consciousness.* By using *trust-allow-dissipate*, you can create whatever realities you want for yourself. It is only a matter of focusing and dedicating time and energy to your vision. Exercise your free will, then just observe as the synchronicities of life take you where you want to be.

Begin by practicing with little problems. Thank them. Trust that life has sent them your way for a reason. Allow the experience of solving them to unfold and appreciate the little gifts you'll take away from it. Then apply the same technique to bigger and bigger problems, should they come. Keep your focus on your vision and the reality you want to build. Repeat and iterate until you find yourself living in a place of peace and serenity with solid foundations. When you find yourself in a place of quiet, a place where your brain has stopped chatting and you can just *be*, that's when you have the blank canvas to start painting the realities you want. You are already indestructible, but now you're going to *feel it*. Then you're going to *live it*. And then you're going to *be it*. You're going to become that peace, and your life will turn into anything you desire, because now you are in control and your life is going to be who and what you really are.

You're no longer just a puppet; you're the puppeteer. And the duality of spirituality is no more. No more spiri*duality*. Just you.

PART III:

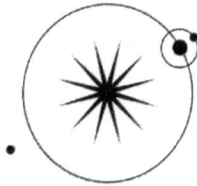

Organizations and Collective Consciousness

11. Navigating a Nonspiritual World

As we've discussed throughout this book, first-person reality is more fundamental than third-person reality. It can't be proven scientifically, but it is a choice that can be made, just like assuming third-person reality is more fundamental has also been just a choice that can't be proven to be right. If we assume first-person reality to be fundamental, though, everything becomes spiritual in nature. The entire universe is spiritual in nature. There is no such thing as a nonspiritual world. Yet, humanity lives as though that's not the case. It has made a very clear choice to believe that third-person reality is more fundamental, more real than anything else and that it is the only thing that matters, even if that can't be proven.

This world perspective can make it really challenging for people who have gained awareness of their own consciousness and existence in first-person reality to coexist with people who have no clue about theirs. I'm not saying it is difficult for spiritual people to live in peace with others. That's actually quite possible and doable. What I'm saying is that it gets more difficult to build a collective third-person reality that is soothing and nice and peaceful and comforting when other consciousnesses (other people) are doing exactly the opposite: building realities that are polarized, black-and-white, and fear-based. We all live and exist in our first-person worlds, which can be made as beautiful and pleasant as we wish regardless of what others do to us, yet we all share just one third-person reality (or, it can be argued, multiple ones, if we do happen to live in a multiverse with parallel realities, but then again, we only experience one of those realities at a time).

There's no easy way to build a spiritual world around us, one where others understand that they are spiritual beings, too. It is much easier for each one of us to independently build a spiritual inner life for ourselves. For some reason, though, we choose, at a consciousness level, to exist as individuals in this time and place in third-person reality, when the vast majority of people are still living like zombies, believing they're dead. Yes, because if you don't know you exist (if you are afraid of dying, for example), that pretty much means you're already dead. It's just a matter of time. People like to be funny by asking, "What would you do in a zombie apocalypse?" Well, it's a wonder that question is even asked. A zombie apocalypse seems to be exactly what we already have, since the choice we make on a daily basis is that third-person reality is more real and fundamental than our own consciousness! Only zombies would believe that.

Because people are so afraid of all sorts of things, they feel the need to protect themselves at all costs. Protect themselves from what, exactly? It doesn't really matter. If there's no real threat, they'll create one! As discussed in part 2, threats are just like problems: they're only there because we put them there. Threats—to our life, to our finances, to national security—feed on and grow from our fears. It's not that there aren't people willing to destroy you and everything else. There are. But you have to understand that you are *indestructible*. There's nothing to fear. And despite the fact that no harm can come to our true selves individually, humanity has been building a story on this planet that is worth preserving and continuing. All of our lives in 3D, our countries, and our planet are worth preserving and worth protecting, *just not from a place of fear*. Fear is behind all the foolishness in this world.

And it's amazing how we use fear as a tool, from parents scaring and projecting their fears onto their kids to governments who manipulate the populace from a place of fear as well. The media, particularly, loves this. It feeds on your fear energy as a vampire would. Our world today is the story of great vampire powers sucking bloodless zombies. It's almost funny! But it could be so much better.

12. The World as a Collective Consciousness Construct

We know by now that third-person reality is a consciousness construct, meaning that it derives from consciousness. Part 2 of this book discussed how we can utilize spiritual concepts to build a better first-person reality for ourselves. By using these concepts, you can really build a beautiful life for yourself, regardless of your third-person circumstances. You don't really need the collaboration or the *will* of anyone else to build your first-person reality. But wouldn't it be so much nicer if we could do it in communion with our fellow consciousnesses (other human beings)? We already live on a beautiful planet, which is part of a beautiful universe (that a greater consciousness may have even built for us, since all comes from consciousness). So why not build a nice collective 3D construct on such a nice planet?

Despite its zombie state, humanity is beautiful in so many ways, too. Despite all our knowledge about the reality of consciousness, it would be a shame if humanity vanished or regressed in third-person reality. Even if we are still at the stage of monkeys with nuclear weapons, we could be so much more. It is worth preserving what we have achieved so we can keep pursuing everything we could be, aiming to reach our full potential. And that means becoming less primal and more spiritual as a whole, as humanity.Those of us learning this for the first time are late in this game. After all, many prophets and spiritual masters have been saying the same things for thousands of years. Maybe we've only come so far because of what they've shown us. Otherwise, we'd probably have destroyed ourselves long ago. So, yes, the spiritual message has been around forever, but today we do face serious existential threats that weren't around thousands of years ago.

Again, these threats are not to be perceived as problems from a place of fear but as opportunities to grow. In this time in our history, there is an opportunity for us to really embrace the spiritual concepts that have been repeated for ages, not just by trying to save a place in heaven when we die but by building heaven on Earth. This is not utopic and unrealistically dreamy anymore. The choice to build heaven on Earth and let go of all fear is ours to make, if we're only willing to. The difference is that before, if we did nothing, humanity would just go on. Today, that's not quite the case. Today we have the ability to destroy the entire planet (multiple times). Eventually, we'll have to make this decision: build heaven on Earth or perish.

I mention in chapter 7 how I wanted to go back to that place of peace in my NDE for several years after my heart attack. Eventually, I started learning how to bring that peace into my life instead. And I am nothing special. If I did it, there's no reason we couldn't build heaven on Earth as a collective, too.

I've mentioned the existential threats. Let's not call them threats, but *negative cocreations*, since everything we perceive as a threat is something that already exists as a possibility in our consciousness space. Here are a few negative cocreations we are already dealing with:

- Global warming and climate change, with ever more violent storms, floods, sea level rise, and scorching temperatures
- Nuclear weapons and other means of mass destruction in the hands of individuals, not just countries (presumably with checks and balances), and transparency-lacking governments all over the world (including ours)
- The malicious or accidental use of AI
- The extreme concentration of wealth by people who are afraid of their nonexistence and who still believe they are what they own or control
- The polarization that could lead the planet into World War III or the U.S. and other democracies into civil war
- The pressures of the current economic school of thought, which is based on unfettered growth on a planet with finite space and resources

For the first time in human history, we are capable of destroying our planet (the only one we have so far) multiple times over. If this list sounds underwhelming, that's because we have been desensitized to these issues and have not been paying attention. The main reason is that these cocreations have developed over the span of a few generations rather than over the lifespan of an individual. From a planetary or historical perspective, though, we can consider that all of these experiments are taking place right now and for the first time ever (as far as our recorded history lets us know).

Nobody can tell when or if an extremely disruptive outcome will result from everything that is going on right now. We simply don't have a historical precedent to assume we know what's going to happen. But the possibility of something catastrophic happening is very real and very here. The fact that everything seems to be fine does not guarantee that things will be fine forever. That actually depends on the choices at a societal level that we are making today. From a historical perspective, anything that happens fifty years from now is already happening, right now. The world is in motion, and nobody knows where it's heading, let alone how to control it. That's why better decisions based on a spiritual, first-person-reality paradigm are in order, because it was our lack of spiritual connection that brought us here in the first place. We didn't need to have these "threats" looming over us (personally, I'd prefer to not have them), but we've chosen to.

It is so clear, and at the same time so little understood: this is all our own creation. *Everything.* All of these negative cocreations come from us and us only. They're not from any external force we need to fear or defend against. It's all us. Each one of us. Each and every one of these challenges started in first-person reality. Because that's simply where all our ideas come from. Everything we build started off as an idea.

Stuff doesn't have ideas. Ideas only exist in consciousness. And if the situations were created by us, we should have the power to solve them as well. How? Certainly not by looking for people to blame or defend against. We are all one and the same. What we need are new and better ideas! Or maybe this is the time to put *very old* ideas into practice.

I truly believe that spiritual ideas are what we need to put in motion a sort of regeneration plan for this planet. All of our problems and negative cocreations come from a lack of spirituality in our lives. The "problem" with spiritual ideas is that they always seem ethereal, intangible, and not really applicable to the "real" third-person world. But the *spiritual* is completely tangible and actionable. The understanding of spiritual reality starts with the simple acknowledgment that our consciousnesses are the manifestation of the universe's spiritual nature. There's nothing ethereal about our consciousness and the emotions we experience in consciousness. Our pain, our love, and our fears are very much real and actionable.

When it comes to the problems and negative cocreations we're all facing, it helps to realize that they're coming from our fears. Think about it. We need more and more because we don't realize we already *are* plenty. We don't actually need stuff to tell others who we are, because what we are is not what we have. Each one of our problems comes from a disconnect with our true self and from believing third-person reality is all there is. It's time to let go of third-person reality *metrics* and focus on first-person *realization*.

We've grown accustomed to the idea that markets will adjust themselves and humanity will "figure it out." We have this thinking that things magically get fixed by themselves, because humanity has been so successful at doing exactly that for such a long time. But we don't have enough good reasons to believe things will just continue to settle by themselves forever; they won't unless we change our mindset and worldview. Actually, we were only able to get here because we managed to change our mindset and worldview over time. And this is a critical time for another big change.

The change is this: we need to stop worshipping third-person reality, with its metrics and goals, as the ultimate reality and realize that our entire lives on this planet are a construct of collective consciousness. Even if matter and 3D could be proven to be fundamental, it's indisputable that our lives, including all the hardship and pain and solidarity and inspiration, are a choice and a construction derived from our own ideas. We can always make better choices and choose a better future. Here, in 3D.

13. The Psychology of Third-Person Reality

Psychology is, to a great extent, a construct of third-person reality. The brain works as a filter that allows for infinite consciousness to have a finite human experience by filtering out all senses, except for five. Other animals have other senses and are able to live different experiences from ours; earlier in this book we discussed dolphins with echolocation and a person with the fictional sense of magnitision as examples. One wonders how many senses and qualia are available to pure consciousness (unfiltered by the brain). It must be incredible. It makes us think of everything we don't even know that we don't know. But here in 3D, we're limited to only five senses and a very noisy brain.

For whatever reason (evolution by natural selection, perhaps), our brain's job is to give us a human experience in 3D. And maybe that's the reason we are not very spiritual as a collective, despite the fact that many of us are choosing to grow spiritually as individuals. As a collective, we're still very much attached to our own third-person reality creation. And the brain is probably behind that phenomenon. The poor brain can't help but try to make sense of all the information it receives from 3D. And because we don't engage as much as we should as a collective in meditation and brain-quieting and shutting down, our lives have become noisier and brainier. The more sensorial stimuli we create as a society the more fascinated we become with third-person reality. Once science became the business of measuring everything, we started believing in all the stimuli and metrics as ultimate (fundamental) reality. If a certain metric tells you you're the best, you believe you're the best. Conversely, if the metrics tell you you're the worst, you also believe in that. You become a loser. The reality being fundamental in first-person, however, means that you can't really be a winner or a loser in a world where there's only you and everything is consciousness, where you are the master of your own reality, and where we are all one and the same. Those distinctions only apply to your *ego*, the psychological identity associated with your physical body, which is not your true self and is meant to eventually die.

The ego is akin to your identity as an individual in society, and it can die even if the body continues. If asked who we are, most of us will give ego-oriented answers, like "My name is X, I'm married to Y, and I'm a parent to XY1 and XY2; I work at company C in position P, and I follow religion R; I'm originally from this town, but now I call this other place home." And so on. None of that is who we truly are. All of those qualifications are anchors that help us make sense of our existence in this 3D world.

I've had the opportunity to go through several ego-killing and reconstructing experiences. At some point in my life, I was Daniel, married to C, parent to DC1 and DC2, Brazilian, a neurologist, and an entrepreneur in health tech. Those were my anchors. Then I decided to migrate to the U.S. I made a self-petition for a green card via the "extraordinary ability" category and was granted residency. In the U.S., however, I was not a neurologist (ego breakup #1). Then I went through a divorce and was no longer husband to C (ego breakup #2). Then I got my U.S. citizenship, and even though I continue to be a Brazilian (and Italian) citizen, that was a little breakup, too (#3). After several years running from a distance the company I had started in Brazil, I felt that it was time for me to start a new career in the U.S. Not having the same business network I had in Brazil, starting another company was not as straightforward as it had once been. Living distant from my family, friends, and professional network was also a serious breakup (#4, #5, and #6). I decided to change industries, and eventually landed a job in biotech (an industry breakup, #7). I was again an employee after fourteen years running my own businesses (breakup #8).

Eventually, I was able to build a new identity, but I lived for many years in a kind of limbo, not knowing exactly who I was. It was a painful journey, but it helped me connect with my true self. Instead of finding emotional security in those anchors, I found it again in my first-person spiritual reality. Yes, it helps having those ego anchors back, but the difference is that now I know they're ephemeral and not the real deal. The real deal is discovering your godlike nature and using that as your anchor, similar to the way religious people use Jesus and other symbols as anchors. Being a rational person, though, as much as I like Jesus's teachings and other religious principles, I needed to discover that connection in a nonreligious way.

I'm sharing this story to make the point that we are not our egos. Egos die all the time. We are something much more profound, but we choose to not accept that when we believe we're just our bodies, brains, and egos.

We were not always like that.

One of my hobbies is astrophotography. I love venturing into the desert to take pictures of the night sky. It is a very meditative experience. It is quiet and peaceful. Particularly, there are almost no stimuli at all. Just the stars. It is a very connecting experience, which brings you closer to nature, to the universe, and to your true self. The brain is no longer at full throttle, trying to make sense of every stimulus. It can take the time to relax and step out for a while. In that state, there are no problems, noises, or confusion. There's just being. There was a time when all people had access to that kind of experience.

It's much more difficult to find that experience today than it was ages ago. In our lit-up cities, saturated with overstimulation, everything in 3D seems so real. We're bombarded with propaganda of all sorts. Everyone wants a little bit of our minds and hearts, and we give them away. We start believing in the concept of success from a third-person perspective. Because we've lost the connection with our true selves, we lack a true self-identity, and thus we seek to be above others to prove our worth. No matter what we do, that extreme need to feel special remains. And we keep wanting more and more of whatever it is we associate with being worthy, whether it's money, published papers or books, reputation, you name it. We start living in a polarized reality of best and worst, top and bottom, winner and loser. Because we've lost touch with the nuances of the world, all we can see is black and white. As a result of that process, humanity today is psychologically quite sick.

Because we've lost touch with our true selves, we've become very needy. We *need* to be successful from other people's perspectives, we *need* external validation, we *need* to get rich, we *need* to be the best, we *need* to be at the top, we *need* to win. Naturally, we start achieving those things, creators that we are. If we *need* to be successful, we'll make sure others aren't as successful as we are. If we *lack* the money to have self-esteem, we'll engage with corruption. If we *need* external validation, we're going to game the system so the system will love us. We prefer to protect our reputation rather than preserve the truth. The more successful at this we are, the more we'll want to keep the status quo from changing, even if that would be the most beneficial thing for the collective. Worst of all, as a result, our continued state of fear as a collective keeps us in a vicious cycle of wars, conflicts, and polarization. If we don't let go of fear, we may end up losing everything.

The more detached from Source (or from ourselves) we are, the more we *need*. The consequence of this is that the most spiritually connected people (perhaps the true winners) are ranked lower and lower. If they truly are connected, they won't care, but then we come back to my initial point in part 3: this all makes it more difficult for anyone to build a soothing, nice, peaceful, and comforting third-person reality for everyone. And that's a psychology we need to break, not just for the sake of living in a happier collective and building heaven on Earth, but because the current psychology is simply unsustainable, given all the negative cocreations that are cooking in our collective consciousness oven. It's time to face the fact that we are mentally ill as a collective. And we need help.

14. Mission and Vision

When I realized I was not going to learn anything about consciousness as a brain mapping scientist, I decided to leave academia. Just as there's more to learn about the rainbow by *seeing* it than *studying* it, I decided I was going to learn about life and consciousness by *living* it. I had been very entrepreneurial since early on in my adult life, having created the very first medical website in Brazil in the mid-90s, when I was just starting medical school, but for many years I was only an amateur entrepreneur. My official career was that of a physician and neuroscientist. When I decided to leave academia and switch careers, the natural decision for me was to become a professional entrepreneur. And, because I was so cerebral and methodical, I decided to pursue a third graduate degree by doing an MBA, which I did at the Wharton School at the University of Pennsylvania.

Wharton was both easy and challenging. From an academic perspective, it was easy. Business was definitely not neuroscience. The concepts and ideas were tangible and pragmatic. Yet, the values in that world were very different from the values in academia. In academia, it was all about your ego. It didn't matter if you didn't make much money; all that mattered was peer recognition and admiration, usually fueled by the number and impact of your scientific papers. In the MBA program, things were more like the "real" world: the only thing that mattered was money. The richer you got, the more successful you were.

In the beginning, there was a shock resulting from the two sets of values clashing within me. I tended to consider academic values more "noble," because they were not money-oriented. With time, though, I came to realize that, be it money or peer recognition, it all boiled down to ego. Whether the currency was money or papers, you had to become rich in that currency to be considered successful. Even if academia considered itself more aspirational and idealistic, its metrics were still very much rooted in third-person reality.

But the MBA program taught me certain concepts that I came to find quite valuable in my life: ideas like leadership, vision, and mission. And it consolidated in me the understanding that money makes the world go 'round. If you want to change anything in third-person reality, money is a language that everybody understands. Poor ideas with lots of demand are much more likely to succeed than good ideas with little demand. I also learned a lot about what drives people and markets, what motivates people to pay for products or services. Through this course of study, I learned a whole lot about human beings and human nature, even though I was already a doctor.

Indirectly, I realized that corporations are consciousness collectives. One of the roles of a CEO or business leader is to build a culture that motivates people and aligns them with a very clear mission and vision. As I was able to experience in practice as the founder and CEO of a health-tech startup, companies are living, conscious entities. Even if we can't perceive it directly, as we do with our own first-person consciousness, the culture of a company is something every collaborator can *feel* in the air. Even if it's not written anywhere, the culture guides decision-making. All of a sudden, you're no longer making your own decisions and following your own nature and *will*. You're following the *will* of a consciousness that is not yours, but of which you are a member.

The thing about a collective consciousness is that, once you let it absorb you and if it's strong enough, you won't behave as yourself anymore. If you are not naturally already aligned with that collective, you may have to decide between aligning yourself with it—with its values, culture, and vibration—or remain in a dissonant state, which can be painful. Many times, that decision process happening within you can be totally subconscious. But if the collective ends up resonating with its followers, that bond can be so strong that people will go to great extremes to preserve that connection, even if it means breaking up with their own greatest core values. That happens for several reasons, most of them based on some sort of lack in their own lives and disconnect with their true selves. The most common is the *need* for money and the *fear* of being money-deprived (i.e., losing the job), but that's not even close to the most important reason.

As conscious individuals, we know we belong to something bigger, a collective consciousness. But because of our disconnect, not the least of which involves living in busy, noisy, bright cities that make us believe that all that exists is third-person reality, we get so disconnected from the spiritual that we end up connecting with the closest collective consciousness available. That could be a sports team, a social group, a political party, a company, or a religious congregation. That connection is so important to us that we will go to great extremes, including evil ones, to foster it and make sure we belong to that group. It gives us *identity* and *meaning*. This is not necessarily a bad thing. Our need for connection is absolutely real and authentic. And connecting with a sports team or a corporation can be a gratifying and positive experience. But it can also be quite negative (think of fighting between different team supporters in Britain or Brazil, for example).

Anyway, the point here is that collective consciousness, which is a spiritual construct, matters and is extremely important for us here, in our very practical and "real" 3D lives. So, if we are to break up with current third-person-reality psychology, we need to transform our various forms of human congregation. Instead of adapting ourselves to comply with what organizations or institutions expect from us, we should try and make our groups more similar to what we truly are and believe ourselves to be. Instead of fearing losing the connection with the collective by trying to change it, we should see ourselves as strengthening our connection with the collective by bringing it closer to who we are. By doing so, we're more likely to have healthier organizations that better resonate with their individual members. This is true for corporations, sports teams, nonprofit organizations, academic institutions, and governments— and not only for politicians but all public servants.

This can start with each one of us in any of the forms of collective consciousnesses we participate in. And transform them we can, because organizations are living, conscious things. Just as unbalanced and nonaligned cells and organs of the body will create diseases, groups whose members' core values are not aligned will also become dysfunctional, bringing imbalance, pain, and suffering to the group and the world it interacts with. That's why bringing organizations closer to ourselves and making them better aligned with our true selves as members will result in better institutions and a better world around them. We don't need to become diseases within organizations to show that we exist and that we're looking for alignment. We can simply be a symptom by having our voice heard.

One way to become a driving force for change within the groups we participate in is to bring up the spiritual aspects that are already acknowledged by all, including their top leadership. Mission and vision are good examples. These are not to be seen as statements to make organizations *look* good. They are to be taken as statements that guide and require organizations to *do* good. And that should be enforced and taken very seriously by participating individual members.

15. Conscious Organizations

Organizations want and need third-person reality in order to prosper. This is true for practically any kind of organization, but from now on I'll be focusing more on corporations, because corporations are the types of organizations that tend to have the most impact on our lives. You may think that governments are the organizations that impact our lives the most, and maybe that was the case once, but most of the change in our modern world is promoted by corporations.

A reliance on third-person reality is a matter of a corporation's survival. That organizational culture, which is collective consciousness, is as willing to live as we are as individuals. These groups actually depend more on third-person reality than individuals do. Companies and other types of organizations manifest through branding and buildings and mechanics (processes, logistics, etc.) that are very much physical and thus fragile. Conscious individuals, however, don't depend on third-person reality as much (even if they believe they do), for their primary and fundamental existence is in first-person reality. Even if the *ego* dies, the reality-generating consciousness of the individual remains.

Organizations, on the other hand, are an interesting mix. In a sense, they're like machines, things that transform an input into an output. But their operations are supported by conscious beings, which form a culture and a collective consciousness. Take conscious beings out of the equation and it's no longer an organization; all you're left with is an engine.

Most often, organizational culture is something that comes from the top—the leadership. The building blocks of a culture start with the organization's mission and vision, which are first-person in nature. See how interesting this is: *mission* and *vision* do not happen in third-person reality. There's no such thing as mission and vision in the laws of physics. A conventional machine, like a car, has no mission or vision. Yet companies can also be seen as sorts of machines that are guided by mission and vision. In that sense, companies and organizations exist in first-person reality, too. The *idea* of an organization only exists in first-person reality and can only be grasped by conscious beings.

Since organizations are living and conscious things, they can and should be part of any strategy aimed at improving our third-person-world reality. It doesn't help to work on ourselves and become better people if we don't make the organizations in our lives part of the process as well. By changing and improving one leader's worldview and mindset (by helping them think within the first-person reality paradigm, for example), we would allow tens or hundreds or thousands of the people who follow that leader to also think in first-person reality terms.

Leadership is always capturing cultural trends from society and incorporating them into the organization. For example, diversity in the workforce was not a movement initiated by leadership; it was initiated by thinkers in society and in the workforce who started disseminating a new understanding. As the idea gained more popularity, leaders embraced it. What was previously taboo becomes accepted and commonplace because of the simple fact that top leadership has assimilated a new idea. The same can happen with the idea that a company has consciousness and exists in first-person reality. As more and more people embrace their own spirituality, corporations and their leadership will follow suit. And the world around the organization will get better.

Religion is not typically discussed in a company for a series of good reasons. Unfortunately, that has also kept spirituality out of the conversation, because there's been so much overlap and confusion between the two ideas. A lot has changed, though. Today, organizations are much more open to discussing subjects such as wellness, mental health, empathy, and mindfulness, just to mention a few spiritual concepts. In fact, many organizations today promote in-office breathing, meditation, and mindfulness sessions and sometimes even a dedicated space where people can go during working hours to participate in those practices. But given the specific challenges humanity is going through now, with all those negative cocreations looming, more is required. And organizations can become leaders in the transformation our 3D world sorely needs.

16. A New Type of Organization

Now that we understand that organizations are conscious entities, for the simple fact that they result from the interactions of many conscious beings (and we can even *feel* an organization's culture in the air), it is time to deepen our understanding of the spiritual nature of organizations and groups. Since organizations do exist to a great extent in first-person reality (through concepts like mission, vision, and others, which can only make sense to beings with consciousness), organizations are, by nature, spiritual entities. If people are spiritual beings, it follows that a collection of people would be spiritual in nature as well.

Organizations can no longer avoid their spiritual role in the world by pretending they have nothing to do with the challenges we face as humanity—those challenges we've created ourselves by using constructs like... organizations. Spirituality is not like religion, which is practiced by each individual in their own free time of their own accord. Spirituality is not even a matter of faith; it's a matter of fact. Spirituality is inescapable for organizations because it's the very essence of their own nature. Organizations cannot walk away from their social responsibility by simplistically and barely abiding by laws and market rules, as if they were merely machines with no sense of consequence or responsibility. The right of organizations to exist in the collective consciousness construct that third-person reality is should be *earned*. I'm not talking about enacting laws and rules to decide which organizations have merit or the right to exist; I'm talking about participating members in organizations, including leadership, no longer accepting their entities acting and behaving in ways that are not aligned with the best interests of our collective consciousness, including our planet and everything else that originally came with it.

So, what exactly would be a *spiritual organization*? Well, let's begin with the basics.

Awareness of Pain

For starters, a spiritual organization recognizes pain. Plain and simple. We've been using pain in this book as clear and indisputable evidence that we live in a first-person reality that exists on top of our third-person world. It may be a very basic concept, but it is also a deeply spiritual one. Only conscious beings can feel pain. So, the first step for an organization that wants this world to survive (and to survive in it) is to accept the existence of pain. It needs to *formally* understand that it can both cause pain and alleviate pain in others, both in its own members and in society more broadly. Every company or organization should understand the pain that it causes or alleviates, and it should hold itself accountable for it.

Separation, Polarization, Conflict, and Competition

Separation is the idea that we are a *creation* of God, or Source, a creation that is separated from the creator. As discussed in part 2, as we create third-person reality from consciousness, we may be led to see ourselves as separated from Source. The idea of life in 3D is to experience this spiri*duality*, which never lets us know for sure if we are creators or creation. Whether this is by design or not, it is a beautiful construction that allows us to exert our *free will*. By getting more spiritual, we gain greater awareness of the *creator* aspect of ourselves. We decrease our separation, and that helps us let go of the fears, uncertainties, and anxieties that are so characteristic of life in third-person reality. With that, we also decrease polarization, conflict, and competition.

It doesn't make much sense for humans as individuals to better themselves by decreasing separation from Source and lessening polarization and conflict in their lives if they continue to work for or participate in organizations that use all of that as means. In that sense, our organizations are lagging way behind. To overcome the challenges we're facing as humanity, we need organizations to catch up.

My first job after Wharton was as a business development executive for a big hospital in São Paulo, Brazil. Despite the fact that the hospital was a nonprofit organization with a very clear mission, it operated on the same basis as a for-profit corporation: *it believed in competition.* And I believed in it, too! Part of my job as the person responsible for the institution's strategic planning was to study the market movements and initiatives of our competitors, as if the whole thing was a great chess game whose strategy was not designed around the best interests of the patient.

Looking back and using the perspective on life that I have now, it's clear to me that the third-person reality we were building around that institution was quite off, to say the least. Here we had a nonprofit hospital whose mission was to save lives worrying about grabbing as many patients as possible from other hospitals who also wanted to save lives. It's a little hard for me to make sense of that these days, because it was not always about being the best; it was about playing a conflict-based game, which involved ways of motivating doctors that were not of the best energy or patient interest.

Don't get me wrong. An individual or organization striving to do or be its best is a laudable thing. And looking at what others are doing in order to optimize your efforts and offer something better, different, or innovative in comparison is extremely beneficial for society. That's what I'd call healthy competition—which is not really competition, because it isn't coming from a place of lack, need, or conflict. You're just trying to do your best. What happens in many cases, though, is that organizations will start obsessing about competitors, seeing that relationship as some sort of war or conflict that necessarily requires one winner. That can still benefit society to some extent, but those wars do not necessarily elevate the vibration of our entire humanity construct, which makes it hard to tell whether the cost or the benefit of conflicting competition is actually bringing some overall net positive value for all.

If the goal of a hospital is to save lives, it should only welcome the help of other organizations interested in helping society achieve that goal. As an organization, we wanted to be the *best* hospital. Once again, there's that third-person reality metric. It would have made sense if the hospital was simply a machine, but as discussed earlier in this chapter, hospitals, like other organizations, aren't anything like that. Hospitals are conscious beings with a culture and a soul. If you want to be the *best* hospital, that can still be a great goal, but all you have to do in that case is continue to improve yourself as an institution. There's no need to worry about competition and creating this false problem. Because that's what competition is: a *non-problem*.

There can still be very good reasons to understand what other hospitals are doing. If another hospital in the region has become a great provider in the oncology space, for example, you may choose to focus on another therapeutic area, because oncology is already covered and solved for. Or you may understand that you can innovate and provide even better services than those of the other hospital. The difference lies in where you're coming from and therefore what type of idea you're communicating down the managerial chain. You can convey the idea that your hospital needs to *win* over the competition, or you can convey the idea that it can *do and be better*, perhaps using the competition as a model but never as an enemy or antithesis. Third-person reality manifests from first-person emotions. If you develop emotions toward a competitor, *feeling the need to beat them*, that only makes that other entity ever more present and alive in your third-person reality. Your competitors become your own creation because you keep feeding and empowering them.

If we want our organizations to exist in a better world, we should make use of better first principles as well. Instead of using the *need to win over competition* as a first principle, the hospital could operate according to the idea that *improving every day* helps save more patients, regardless of what others are doing. One idea comes from *lack*. We *need* to win, because we're not winners already and we're not enough. The other comes from *excitement*. If we put in the effort and do the work, we get better at achieving our goals. And if people join our organization because they *believe* (again, a first-person-reality and spiritual concept) in the organization's mission, vision, and goals (i.e., its spiritual values), nothing can make them more excited and productive. And that makes all the difference in the world. The third-person reality created by an organization is the sum of the third-person realities created by every individual contributor. The energy an organization's leaders communicate and use to motivate its contributors to participate in that construct matters. A lot.

Despite our example of a health care organization, which is supposedly an altruistic space by nature, make no mistake: health care is an industry like any other. The points made here are true not only for hospitals but for any type of organization in our 3D world that makes use of conscious beings. They are true for any kind of endeavor.

Managing What Can't Be Measured

A maxim of business administration is what can't be measured can't be managed. While that is true in our third-person, scientific reality, our organizations continue to be run by conscious beings, whose consciousnesses are not computable or measurable. First-person, conscious reality is an experiential reality. No matter how much our technology evolves, we'll never be able to measure a person's conscious experience of being part of an organization. Even if every person were replaced with an AI agent, it's still likely that eventually those agents would start giving way to some sort of AI consciousness (just like our brains do), which we might have no idea how to connect with or relate to compared to our fellow humans.

Of course, just like with the brain, you can measure *correlates* of your organization's members' conscious experience (employee satisfaction surveys come to mind), but that doesn't tell you the full story. Specifically, you can't tell what goes on in the first-person realities of your organization's people—the organization's collective consciousness. That's something you can't measure. At any time, the organization is a real-time construct of what's going on in the inner realities of everyone involved with it. You can't measure it, but you can still see (or *feel*, from your own first-person perspective) the collective manifestation of the many people in your organization unfold around you.

Even though you can't really measure first-person realities, you surely can manage them, particularly because you are also a conscious being and you can relate. In that sense, what can't be measured can still be managed. Because everything in our 3D world comes from first-person constructs, perhaps the most important thing top management should oversee is exactly that: people's first-person realities. If people feel vibrationally aligned with the organization, that vibration will add to the organization's vibration, creating resonance.

On the other hand, when people are not vibrationally aligned, meaning that they're not focusing on manifesting a reality that is aligned with their leaders' vision, their individual vibrations will contribute to canceling out the overall organization's vibration, creating dissonance. I know, "vibration" is a very vague and ethereal concept, but at the same time, it isn't. Right? As conscious beings, we get the idea. We can tell the difference between a meeting at the company that has a positive energy/vibration and one that has a negative energy/vibration. It's an idea an unconscious computer would never be able to grasp.

So, how do you manage your contributors' conscious creation, which you'd like to be aligned with yours? It starts from your own consciousness, naturally. It's not about measuring people; it's about *connecting* with people. When people are connected to you and to each other at a consciousness level, you, your contributors, and your organization are all in *flow*. People start anticipating each other's moves like they could read each other's minds. That's the essence of a team. A true team harmoniously behaves as a single entity. If you don't have the feeling in your organization of operating as a single entity, there is some *spiritual alignment* work to be done (or *consciousness alignment*, if that terminology makes you feel more comfortable). What matters is that the state of flow of cohesive consciousness collaborating toward an end is something that you can only *feel* in first-person reality. It's not available for you to measure.

The type of energy used to align the people in an organization can vary. It is totally possible, for example, to use fear-based energies to create alignment and cohesiveness. As a matter of fact, that's exactly what ends up happening in many corporations and organizations (and governments). In that case, people aren't reading each other's minds to build flow and get goals accomplished. If they're all of the same negative energy, they'll be reading each other's minds with the objective of winning in a corporate survival-of-the-fittest kind of game. This is a game being played right now in many types of organizations, from nonprofits to corporations to governments. It's a game with many "winners," who are usually the most fear-driven individuals. The winner is rarely the organization itself or the world around it.

Work Hard, Play Hard

When you master the idea of consciousness cohesiveness in an organization, some other concepts start making less sense. Hard work is a measurable thing, which means it belongs to third-person reality. As we've been discussing, however, third-person realities are not self-generated. Third-person realities originate in the first-person realm. Therefore, first-person-reality emotions such as passion, creativity, originality, and others are the real reality-creation driving forces.

Most of all, the cohesiveness of the reality-creating vibrations of multiple people is unbeatable, because when people find themselves in that kind of flow, working never *feels* hard or painful; it is always enjoyable, even if it is hard. There's no way that believing work or play should be hard will create a positive reality, for either the worker or the organization. It might even create a big and admired and impactful reality (in third-person-reality metrics), but that doesn't mean it will be positive and joyful. (As a matter of fact, many old-school bosses would prefer it that way.) As a result, organizations that believe in no-pain-no-gain as a means to success are most likely fueling the threats we currently face as humanity, and the prophecies of our negative cocreations will become self-fulfilling. Once again, it's all our creation. Pain, as a first-person reality experience can indeed create gain in third-person reality, but that's a costly way to obtain gain. Excitable work and excitable play is what creates equally excitable realities and outcomes.

Profits and Returns on Investment

Finally, we can't finish the discussion on the *new type of organization* without discussing the financial reality of the third-person realm. From the get-go, it's important to say that money is not evil. As with anything else in objective reality, money is neutral. It is we who *attach* value and meaning to money. In and of itself, money can be a very useful metric and tool. It attaches value to things to inform us what is easiest or hardest to manifest in 3D. In that sense, money is quite informative. It also shows us how valuable the output of our own work and creation is to other people. So far, so good.

The problem with money is that, being such an obvious and readily available *metric*, it is adopted by most people as a way to make a bogus measurement of someone's worth. We've even incorporated that idea into our language: "John is worth a million dollars." What does that even mean? If John gets sick, should we all run a crowdsourcing campaign to raise a million dollars to save him, because that's what he's worth? Attributing numbers to people is a fruitless idea. As if allowing money to represent a measurement of someone's true self-worth weren't bad enough, it creates all sorts of perverse incentives! Nobody enjoys feeling less than someone else. And if they are not well-rooted in their spirituality, they'll do whatever it takes to look good in that metric. Or they'll feel depressed and victimized. Neither outcome is good. And that creates all sorts of negative realities for all of us, with lots of conflict and polarization, ultimately leading to the negative cocreations we've been discussing.

One might argue that money can be an incentive for people to create great things. While that's probably true, it's not always enough to counterbalance these negative effects. Because of the association of the money metric with a person's worth, the result is a whole lot of misguided incentives, including corruption. Yes, people may have accomplished great deeds for the simple fact that they wanted to have more money, but in a more spiritual society, self-fulfillment would have been a much more powerful and gratifying driver.

Self-fulfillment is something that can actually be perceived and experienced in first-person reality, whereas money is an external representation of an inner reality that doesn't really exist without self-fulfillment. By itself, money is not fulfilling. It's not really part of us. It only exists outside of us as a third-person-world metric. What we do to create money can indeed be very fulfilling. But if the focus is on the *number* that money measures rather than on the *experience* that fulfills us, then people will take on whatever unfulfilling stratagems they can think of as long as that brings them money. And this drags everyone else around them into that unfulfilling dynamic. Instead of building great third-person realities together, we find ourselves struggling with separation, conflict, and polarization.

What's really needed are organizations and societal agreements that promote and optimize true individual and collective fulfillment. But that's not what we have. What corporations are required to provide is return on investment for shareholders, not great deeds, achievements, or fulfillment. It's not really the corporations' fault. It is the fault of all of us, of our entire third-person-reality construct. Instead of dedicating our creative energy and work life to the creation of better and fulfilling realities for ourselves, we delegate that energy to money, something that doesn't really exist. We want money to work for us, as if working was a bad and shameful thing. Work is supposed to be a fulfilling and expressive activity, not the kind of thing we should run from. Work is the means by which we imprint our conscious expression in 3D. It is a nice way to tell other people in 3D that we exist. But instead we choose to delegate that to money, so it can do the work for us while we keep engaging in ever more meaningless pursuits.

I'm not alone in saying that profits shouldn't be a corporation's ultimate purpose. There was a time our jobs had meaning and were fulfilling. A shoemaker, for example, would be proud of their creation. One's craft or trade created identity (to the point of becoming a surname in many cultures) and produced a fulfilling experience. But when people, suffering from feelings of lack and inferiority on the inside, focus on making money just for the sake of having more than others, they end up creating a reality distortion field that breeds negativity and misguided incentives into the world. Instead of pride, this leads to resentment and polarization.

Of course, there are good reasons for people to decide to focus on money as an end rather than as the outcome of a fulfilling activity. And the way the world is set up today, pursuing your passion doesn't always lead to a financially comfortable life. Establishing a fair set of incentives and disincentives around money creation and accumulation has been always a challenge for humankind. There's no perfect system and there will never be as long as we keep insisting on interpreting third-person reality as *fundamental.*

This is not about promoting socialism or reframing our political or economic systems. It's not that capitalism is failing us. Capitalism is a third-person construct; it can't be at fault for anything. The fault is ours, a consequence of our separation and lack of connection with our spirituality. We've transferred gratification to third-person reality, forgetting that gratification can only happen in consciousness—in other words, at a spiritual level. Capitalism is just a system. Like any other system, it can be used in positive or negative ways. And it is often used in very positive ways! Capitalism is a way to organize and set certain ideas and ideals in motion. It is a means to an end, but we've subverted the system by turning it into an end in itself. No longer are we making money as a consequence of fulfilling activities. Money has become the goal in and of itself, and an empty and purposeless one, at that.

So, what is the *new type of organization's* role in all of this? First, we as humanity should internalize and pass on the idea that a corporation is a living, conscious entity with a purpose. From the individual contributor consciousness level to the all-encompassing organizational culture, companies exist first and foremost to manifest in 3D the creation that began as ideas and ideals. That's where the worth of a company and its people reside. If the result of that creation won't make certain investors happy, then perhaps it is time to educate them and spread these ideas, so that the company can find investors that are better aligned with what the company truly is and creates. I've had the experience of running a startup with investors that were not entirely aligned with the company's purpose. It was not a good deal.

Any company is better off sticking to its core, first-person-reality values and principles, the mission and vision that bring its people together, to manifest whatever that collective has the *will* to do. Companies are conscious entities, and it doesn't serve any company well if its goal is to make people richer just for the sake of it. Giving returns to investors should be just a natural consequence of a company's pursuing its purpose according to its spiritual (first-person) principles.

17. Building a Joyful World

The spir*iduality* of our lives is a real thing, not only on a personal level but also on a societal level. We tend to think that spiritual connection is something for each one of us to develop independently and alone. The world is so broken that we may feel embarrassed to discuss these ideas outside of a very close circle of friends and family members. We don't want to jeopardize our jobs by bringing this type of conversation to the workplace. Yet, the lack of a broader open discussion on spirituality is hindering the collective spiritual progress of the entire planet, as well as the progress of many of us individually. It is more difficult to develop a spiritual life for ourselves when others around us are still so detached from it. Our organizations, governments, and institutions could be doing a much better job.

When I started writing this book, I had no idea I was eventually going to bring organizations and corporations to the discussion. This was supposed to be a spiritual initiation book. But then I realized that improving ourselves individually and simply moving on with our lives was not enough. At least, not for me. The spreading effect of spiritual ideas would be much greater if those ideas were adopted at the organizational and societal levels. After all, we use organizations to structure everything else in our lives. These collective entities are our own creations, and they represent us. So, for us to be properly represented as spiritual beings sharing a human experience on Earth, institutions have to become part of the equation, too.

It's my hope that by combining the ideas for individual spiritual growth with the concept of conscious and spiritual organizations, we can create a multiplier effect that will result in a third-person reality that is joyful and fulfilling for all.

Conclusion

This book was not originally intended as a self-help book (although part 2 can be used that way), but more as a humanity-help book. It is true that the best way to fix the world is by fixing ourselves first. Maybe by fixing ourselves we start vibrating with a version of reality that is already better, so we don't actually need to fix anything in the world at all. We just shift to a version of the world that is already better aligned with us. (And if parallel realities exist, then consciousness may have the ability to shift its focus to different realities according to its state of being.)

That said, the world as it exists today needs tons of help. There are still too many people mesmerized by third-person reality and its metrics, obsessing about achieving dominance and power goals without taking notice of who they already are. They try to feel godlike by imposing themselves over others without realizing that God doesn't even do that. This is so much wasted opportunity.

This initiation book on spirituality was written as an invitation. There's so much more to learn, and each one of these chapters could be expanded into entire books just about those specific subjects. There's a movement out there led by people who are going through their own spiritual journeys and transformations. More and more people are waking up to spiritual reality and building their lives around spiritual values. Countless books have been written on the subject. It is a real thing! No matter what religion you follow or faith you hold close to your heart, I want you to have spir*iduality* in your life. And I hope this book can help you build a better life for yourself and those around you.

If this book has found you, I'd like to invite you to keep connected. Join the Spir*iduality* community at www.spiriduality.com and keep growing your understanding of first-person reality. I'd be delighted to see you there.

About the Author

Does the brain create consciousness or does consciousness create the brain? If consciousness creates the brain, which is the idea that I develop in this book, then who I am is one and the same as who you are. If consciousness creates the brain, it is likely non-computable and thus nondivisible. We're all the same. Whichever alternative is right, the fact is that we're living beings on a journey.

My journey started in Salvador, Brazil, where I was born, and continued in Porto Alegre, Brazil, where I was raised. Since I was very young, I wanted to understand how the brain creates consciousness. I became a physician and a neurologist. Then a postdoctoral neuroscientist at Harvard, where I developed brain maps to help guide epilepsy and brain tumor surgeries. When I finally realized that I was never going to understand consciousness by studying the brain, I decided to just live and experience life. I did an MBA at Wharton and became an entrepreneur. Today, I live in San Diego, CA, where I help build and grow science-backed companies.

Spiriduality is the result of a lifetime quest around understanding who we truly are. As someone who went through a profound spiritual journey after a near-death experience, and having lived in academia as a scientist and in the more concrete business world as a consultant and entrepreneur, I felt the need to share what I've learned from all those different walks of life, including different countries and cultures. We're living turbulent times, and building a deep understanding of our true spiritual nature is pivotal for us to overcome the challenges ahead. I hope that by developing the notion of spiriduality we'll be better prepared to navigate a world that seems ever more complex and uncertain, but which, in reality, only gets more and more fascinating.

www.spiriduality.com

www.ingramcontent.com/pod-product-compliance
Lightning Source LLC
LaVergne TN
LVHW041221080426
835508LV00011B/1027